'Living purposely allows us to be the person we want to be. Tim Hebert provides a pathway which shows that anything is achievable when we act and lead with intention. Why would we settle for anything less?'

Michael Black, President, MJB Associates

'A provocative call to action that drives leaders to deep introspection. When today's leaders look for something to guide them, I hope they find Tim's book as their compass.'

David Flink, CEO, Eye to Eye and 2021 CNN Hero

'In sharing his own transformational journey of cultivating self-awareness, self-inquiry, and growth-oriented practices, Tim Hebert shows how becoming an "intentional leader" can help you and your organization navigate challenges and opportunities and rise to any circumstance.'

Pam & Scott Harper, Business Advancement Inc., and co-hosts
of 'Growth Igniters® Radio'

'*The Intentional Leader* is all about effective professional relationships. Blending relevant research with lived experiences, Tim Hebert provides a blueprint for those who aspire to enlightened leadership – and to the successful business outcomes that flow from it.'

Mildred Hastbacka, PhD, founder, Prakteka LLC, and
author of Channeling Wisdom

'*The Intentional Leader* provides a roadmap for becoming the person that others want to follow.'

Pam Hyland, CEO, Girl Scouts of Southeastern New England

'Tim Hebert's powerful book will transform your core beliefs on leadership. Hebert provides insight on reinventing your purpose and creating "unguarded moments" to unleash your very own leadership superpower.'

Chris Jann, Founder and CEO, Medicus IT

'The concepts of Decisive, Defining, and Unguarded moments will help you understand the difference between ordinary effort vs. finding your always in-the-moment intentional self. *The Intentional Leader* is a must-read!'

Raju Chekuri, President & CEO, Netenrich, Inc., and
founder & Chairman Opsramp, Inc.

'*The Intentional Leader* provides a powerful roadmap to enable people to intentionally develop their leadership presence and inevitably create success personally and professionally.'

> Paul Cronin, CEO, Apogee IT Services, and Leadership
> Challenge Certified Facilitator

'*The Intentional Leader* is packed with rich content that includes practical tools for building and improving leadership success ... along with candid, humble leadership lessons shared by the amazing Tim Hebert. It's a must-read for leaders at any stage in their journey.'

> Marianne Caserta, VP of Finance Transformation, NWN/Carousel

'A powerful step-by-step guide to how a deep understanding of self can translate to next-level leadership.'

> Ankit Mahadevia, MD, co-founder and CEO, Spero Therapeutics

'*The Intentional Leader* unquestionably raises the game for leaders, from emerging to highly experienced, by diving deeper into self-awareness and unleashing one's inner authority. A must-read for leaders aspiring to greatness!'

> William F. Hatfield, Bank of America Rhode Island President (retired)

'Tim enlightens the reader to embrace the notion that leadership is not an outward-focused discipline, but is instead one that begins as an intentional inward-focused practice that can manifest in big ways personally and professionally.'

> Chris Poe, Staff Vice President – Manager,
> Cloud Infrastructure Services

'A personal account of why and how self-awareness can benefit our professional and personal lives.'

> Carlos Fuentes, President, Axiom Actuarial Consulting

'Brilliant and truly eye-opening.'

> Todd Cronin, VP of Business Development, CE Tech, LLC

'A must-read for anyone who aspires to attain their peak powers as a leader. Hebert teaches us not only how to stay accountable to our vision, but how to bring our core values into our daily operations and make leadership decisions from a place of deep integrity, not expediency.'

> Chip Conley, author of Wisdom at Work and
> founder of Modern Elder Academy

THE
INTENTIONAL
LEADER

How inner authority can
unleash strong leadership

TIM HEBERT

BLOOMSBURY BUSINESS
LONDON • OXFORD • NEW YORK • NEW DELHI • SYDNEY

BLOOMSBURY BUSINESS
Bloomsbury Publishing Plc
50 Bedford Square London WC1B 3DP UK
29 Earlsfort Terrace, Dublin 2, Ireland

BLOOMSBURY, BLOOMSBURY BUSINESS and the Diana logo are trademarks
of Bloomsbury Publishing Plc

First published in Great Britain 2021

A catalogue record for this book is available from the British Library

Library of Congress Cataloguing-in-Publication data has been applied for

ISBN: HB: 978-1-4729-9007-5; eBook: 978-1-4729-9008-2

2 4 6 8 10 9 7 5 3 1

Typeset by Deanta Global Publishing Services, Chennai, India
Printed and bound in Great Britain by CPI Group (UK) Ltd, Croydon CR0 4YY

To find out more about our authors and books visit www.bloomsbury.com
and sign up for our newsletters

To Kim

'Only from the heart can you touch the sky' – Rumi

Contents

Introduction

When I was in my second year of high school, my class was assigned to read Ralph Waldo Emerson's essay, 'Self-Reliance'.

When it was my turn to read aloud, I read this passage: 'Trust thyself: every heart vibrates to that iron string.' I was so struck by these words that I read the sentence over, and over, and over...until the teacher finally snapped and sent me to the principal's office.

As the principal regarded me dubiously, I explained that I hadn't been clowning around; I had just *really* liked that passage. For whatever reason, the idea of 'trust thyself' resonated deeply with me. But as I struggled to put words around what was flying through my head, what became uncomfortably clear was that *I didn't trust myself* – and I had no idea why.

That moment launched a 40-plus-year journey to find that iron string, establish a sense of trust in myself, and forge a connection to what I now refer to as 'inner authority' – a profound, unshakable clarity about who I am and what I value. It also brought me to some of the most influential literature of my life – that of the transcendentalist movement.

This journey has shaped me as a person and as a leader. And it started with a single moment of *awareness*.

There are three kinds of moments that can change our lives and create who we are as leaders. They are:

1. *Decisive Moments,* where we make an intentional choice to do or create something.
2. *Defining Moments*, where we take (or don't take) an action that exemplifies our core character and shows what we are truly capable

of. These moments create others' images of us, and our perceptions of ourselves.

3. *Unguarded Moments,* the moments of inner clarity and stillness when our authentic self manifests in a natural and uncontrolled manner.

Decisive Moments are crucial for leaders because they are like crossroads in our lives and work. Everything that comes after those moments is altered as a result of our choice. Showing up with integrity in our Decisive Moments is what makes us good leaders.

Defining Moments are when we reveal our character – intentionally or otherwise – through our actions. They show others exactly what we are made of, and what we represent. Failure to recognize Decisive and Defining Moments is a huge part of what makes leaders ineffective.

Then, there are Unguarded Moments. Emerson wrote, 'The reason why the world lacks unity, and lies broken and in heaps, is because man is disunited with himself.' When we don't take the time to go within and examine who we know ourselves to be, connect with our Core Ideology, and tap into our inner authority, we will almost always sit down when the world calls us to stand up.

Why? Because it's hard to act in alignment with an ideology you can't define or understand. It's hard to stay true to yourself, your values, your purpose, or your greater vision when you don't fully know who you are, what you stand for, and who you want to become.

Our Unguarded Moments are the times when the deepest core of who we are moves through us to create something beyond what we could have achieved otherwise. The times when we suddenly feel words welling up within us – words that we would never have considered a few moments before. The moments of solitude when a significant and profound sense of knowing comes over us, and we see clearly for the first time something that had previously been ambiguous or inaccessible. The times when our innermost self speaks, and we are quiet enough to listen.

Our Decisive and Defining Moments speak more eloquently than words about who we are and what we value. Our choices and actions can also be our greatest teachers. But we can't access the gifts of our Decisive and Defining Moments without the inner stillness and connection that is the gift of the Unguarded Moment. In fact, the *only* way to intentionally create Decisive and Defining moments is through the gateway of Unguarded Moments. As we'll explore in this book, intentionality is one of the great gifts of self-awareness.

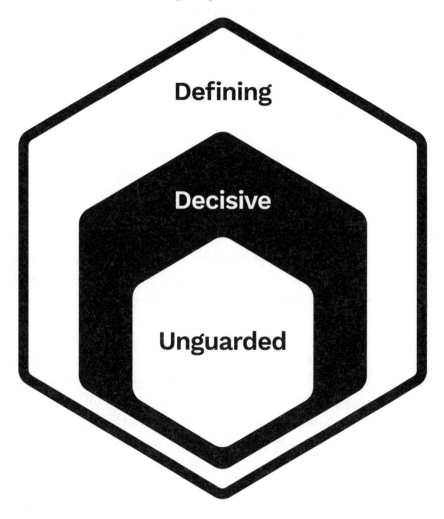

We all have the capacity to experience Unguarded Moments – in fact, most of us do it without even being aware of it! We have moments of inspiration in the shower, or while driving. We have epiphanies while listening to music or watching great films. When we still our minds, deeper wisdom has a way of making itself known.

However, self-awareness gives us the capacity to not only create Unguarded Moments at will, but also to fully assimilate what they have to teach us. We all have a deep reservoir of wisdom inside us. It's part of being human. But, like any other skill, it takes awareness, practice, and dedication to be able to access that state of being at will.

I understand if you're sceptical, but I assure you, this isn't a trip down some philosophical rabbit hole. Inner connection is no longer solely the realm of monks and yogis. It's the path of the Intentional Leader – and it's the *only* way to truly access the confidence, resilience, and self-reliance that you will need to step up as a force for change and growth in your organization, your life, and the world.

Today's leadership crisis

We have an abundance of 'leaders' in our world today. Those who truly stand out are those who lead in a way that inspires others to give their all to a cause – whether that cause is ending world hunger, developing cutting-edge technologies, or selling shoes. I call these people *Intentional Leaders.*

Intentional Leadership is about living and leading with direction, clarity, purpose, and clearly expressed values. It's about being the best version of yourself – being someone whom others want to follow, emulate, and co-create with. It's more than just pushing others towards a goal or commanding social influence; it's about leading from the front of the line, and inspiring others to join you on your journey.

Intentional Leadership is responsive, not reactionary. It's transformational, not transactional. It's positive and inclusive. It lifts people up instead of keeping them down. It's innovative, daring, and inspirational. It's leadership with the long game in mind.

There are a thousand books out there about leadership styles, techniques, and strategies. This isn't one of them. This book will teach you to use self-awareness, self-inquiry, and growth-oriented practices to excavate the leader who is already inside you. When you do this work, you will cultivate a leadership style that is authentic, compelling, and effective. You'll learn how to navigate opportunities and challenges both large and small. If you know who you are, and trust yourself, you will rise to meet any circumstance – and in so doing, leave a legacy far beyond your current title and position.

Before we go further, the first thing I want you to know is that leaders are made, not born. There are no 'natural' leaders. Sure, some people have great charisma or other strengths associated with leadership, but that's not the same thing. Leaders are forged through hard work, practice, commitment, and constant improvement.

Leadership has always been, and always will be, a choice. It's not a strategy; it's a state of being.

Anyone can be a leader, no matter where their natural strengths lie. Skills can be acquired along the way to make the journey easier – such as good communication and team-building techniques – but leadership isn't the province of a few 'chosen ones'. It's a self-selecting field with room for anyone who wants to show up.

The second thing I want you to remember is that there is a vast difference between positional leadership and Intentional Leadership. The first is conveyed by title and hierarchy while the latter is evoked through presence. And when it comes to inspiring others to work towards our goals, the second works far better than the first.

In this book, I will teach you how to become an Intentional Leader using the power of Unguarded Moments, focused self-awareness practices, and human connection. It's an inside-out journey into your genius, and quite possibly not the one you were expecting when you picked up this book. You won't read about leadership 'styles'. You won't see strategies for negotiating a raise or moving up the ladder. But I can promise you that, if you put this information to work wholeheartedly, you will understand more about who you are as a leader, how you can connect with and motivate others, and how you can create more meaningful results than any task-based strategy can deliver.

How to become an Intentional Leader

As you've probably guessed by now, Intentional Leadership is an inside-out proposition. But I don't just teach my clients, mentees, and students how to turn the lens inwards. This book doesn't use a typical 'self-help' approach; it's more deliberate than that. While it's wonderful to know yourself and understand your inner motivators, it's how you *leverage* that knowledge that translates into Intentional Leadership.

This book is a primer on how to take the wisdom we gain through self-awareness and put it to work in our leadership journey. The discussions and exercises I offer are practical and forward-looking, and are intended to create rapid and compounding change.

In Part I of this book, we will look at what Intentional Leadership is, and what it isn't. We'll introduce the concept of Ghost Mode and discuss why and how its symptoms undermine the results we want to achieve as leaders. Then, we'll make a case for self-awareness as the ultimate remedy for Ghost Mode and the entry point into the realm of inspirational, inclusive, *intentional* leadership.

In Part II, we'll explore the four symptoms of Ghost Mode in depth – lack of awareness, lack of trust/reactionism, unhealthy ego, and disconnection – and discuss how each shows up in an individual as well as at an organizational level. I'll also provide the 'antidotes' to each of these symptoms, and show you how each can be accessed and utilized by anyone who desires to be an Intentional Leader, no matter where their strengths lie.

In Part III, we'll put your inner work into action by taking the concepts and practices introduced in Parts I and II and dropping them into real-life leadership situations. I'll provide detailed guidance to help you get your team on board with your vision, set and accomplish goals effectively, ask for and integrate feedback, and make the right choices when challenges arise. Finally, I'll make a case for how Intentional Leadership is the best way for organizations around the world to survive and thrive in the upcoming decades.

As a nod to the man who inspired my journey, each chapter in this book will begin with an inspirational quote from Emerson; these will set the tone for the learning curve of the chapter.

When you turn the last page of this book, you will:

- fully understand the concept of Intentional Leadership;
- understand how Intentional Leadership can improve your outcomes personally and within your organization;
- have an increased awareness of how you are showing up in Decisive, Defining, and Unguarded Moments, and how these shape your leadership style;
- understand the four symptoms of Ghost Mode and how they impact your leadership in ways large and small;
- have developed a solid Core Ideology that includes your values, purpose and vision, and that you can use as a barometer for decision-making in all situations;
- understand the difference between goals and vision, and how to set goals in a way that moves you forwards;
- feel empowered to seek out, receive, and integrate feedback;
- feel more prepared to inspire and empower others as a leader.

The world needs more Intentional Leaders. It's my mission to help you uncover your greatness. I've pursued this goal as a CEO, speaker, and educator, and now as an author. I believe that, once you understand how to create change as a leader by shifting your experience, beliefs, behaviours, and approach, you will create a ripple of change across your organization and the business world that will carry us all into a brighter future.

Part 1

CHAPTER 1

What It Means to Be a Leader

'What lies behind you, and what lies in front of you, pales in
comparison to what lies inside of you.' – Emerson

At 8.45 a.m. on 11 September 2001, I showed up to work as the
no-nonsense, results-driven, 'techie' co-owner and CEO of Atrion, an
information technology (IT) services company. When that day was
over, I was no longer the same person.

Atrion started as a two-person operation running out of a spare
bedroom; over the years, we'd grown from a start-up to a $12 million-
a-year business with 53 employees. Despite the Dot Com bust and the
after-effects of Y2K, we were on a path to exponential growth. I was a
technical leader, and I prided myself on my effectiveness because of the
industry-leading results we were achieving.

The day before, we'd held a leadership development event at the
Warren Center in Ashland, Massachusetts with a new corporate
trainer. After a full day of education, experiential learning, and team
building, everyone was jazzed to get to work and put the things they'd
learned into action. I was just starting my debrief with the facilitator
when several people burst in with the news that two planes had been
flown into the World Trade Center.

We had a 14in TV in one corner; a group of us huddled around
it, open-mouthed, barely breathing. It was hard to process what we
were witnessing on that tiny screen, but the magnitude of what was
happening became more evident with every passing moment.

By 11.00 a.m. that day, I was no longer the same person I had been
just hours before. None of us was. The world suddenly seemed bigger,

scarier, and more screwed up than any of us had realized. All the things that had seemed important yesterday now seemed flimsy and insubstantial. The facilitator I'd been debriefing left in a daze; neither he nor I knew what to say.

I didn't sleep at all that night. I was grieving for the victims and their families, but also consumed with worry about what was going to happen to my company and our 53 employees. Our industry was already in a recession; now, it seemed very likely that the whole world economy would start to nosedive.

I knew that my team would be looking to me for guidance, but I had more questions than answers. What if our country went to war? What if our whole company and everything we'd worked for evaporated, and I could no longer provide for my family? Minute by minute, my uncertainty was growing – and if I was feeling this way, how must my employees be feeling?

'I have to address my team,' I thought. 'And I have to do it tomorrow. Well, today,' I amended, glancing at the bedside alarm clock.

In light of what had just happened, what could I say that would mean anything? How could I make them feel safe when I felt like the ground was sliding out from under my own feet?

A few hours later, I gathered my team, intending to share with them everything that I was thinking and feeling. I didn't want to offer platitudes or a canned 'condolence' speech; nothing I could say in that realm would be enough. Nor did I want to share something purely derivative, tactical, and numbers-driven.

As the moment of my talk approached, I closed my door and tried to calm down and clear my mind. I tried and failed to obtain that inner peace that I so desperately needed. A few minutes later, I stood in front of my team. We observed a tearful moment of silence. As we all stood together, I felt the calm that I had been searching for settle upon me. I felt like someone had turned off the noise inside my head. And suddenly, I knew exactly what I needed to say.

'To be completely honest with you,' I began, 'I have no idea what is going to happen to our world – or in our business, for that matter.

What I do know is that our world changed yesterday, and it's going to get more challenging. We were already facing difficulties with a slowing economy. Yesterday's attack will only accelerate this effect.

'But we've faced difficult times before, and we've not only survived, we've become stronger. I took some time this morning to go back and reflect upon what we did during the last two recessions that helped us to be successful. I came up with a plan that we are going to implement immediately, to make sure our boat doesn't get swamped when things get rough.'

Then I outlined the simple, three-step plan that I believed would carry us through the inevitable storm. First, if *we* were feeling this way, our clients were going through the same stresses. Our job was to get closer to them. Second, we would need to be very frugal for the next couple of years. There would be salary freezes and limited bonuses. There would be no sacred cows; no one would be exempt. Third, we were *not* going to cut to the bone. Instead, we were going to continue to make smart investments – and the best investment Atrion could make as a company was in the people who made it great, every day.

When we wrapped up that meeting, we had a high-level framework for survival that everyone understood and could get behind. Not everyone was happy about it – mainly when it came to the salary freezes – but given what was at stake, our employees knew the gravity of the situation and the sacrifices that would have to be made. For the first time in our company's history, we were connected by a common cause; we would get through this together, or not at all.

That inspirational talk was a Defining Moment in my life. But there was something *more* that occurred – that moment of clarity that descended seconds before I started to speak. It was what I now identify as an Unguarded Moment. I tapped into something completely authentic. I was comfortable with being truthful, vulnerable, and exposed, even in front of my whole team. And something more than I expected came through me.

Before that day, I'd been a talented manager and a good boss. I was great at motivating people to accomplish the task at hand, and I tried to be fair and objective in every situation. But I'd never had to lead people through this level of crisis before. Atrion's very survival depended on how I showed up for my team today, tomorrow, and in the months to come.

9/11 completely shifted my understanding of what it takes to be a leader. Leadership was no longer about numbers or results; that was the easy part. Instead, it was about doing the right thing, setting an example, and being the kind of person whom others wanted to follow. It was doing things that weren't necessarily required on a business level, but which were absolutely needed on a human level. It was about speaking from my heart as well as my head. And, most of all, it was about investing in relationships and empowering everyone to feel like they were a part of the broader vision – like they were co-creating our future.

Over the next 15 months, we lost a massive chunk of our industry. Most of my competitors in the New England area went out of business. Half the people in my network were looking for jobs. And in the same period, Atrion not only survived, but *doubled in size*. We got closer to our clients, discovered their evolving needs and brought them new and innovative solutions. Even during those first challenging months, we only laid off three people – two contractors whose terms expired at the end of the year, and one employee we'd already been planning to phase out.

How did we do it? Everyone pitched in and brought their best to the job. But that wave of dedication started on the day I decided to show up as a *leader*, not just a manager. We leaned on our Core Ideology – our shared values, purpose, and vision, which were contained in the framework I had proposed on 12 September. We placed greater importance on relationships than on numbers. And we collectively invested in a company culture that focused on making a difference over growing the bottom line.

* * *

The real reason why leadership fails in so many organizations isn't a lack of resources, or a poorly trained team, or the economy, or any other external factor. Leadership fails *from the inside out* due to a lack of presence and self-awareness. When leaders know and understand themselves, their motivations, and their blind spots, they can be more decisive. They can get people on board with their visions, and create innovative solutions to what at first appear to be insurmountable problems. In other words, they become more than managers. They become Intentional Leaders.

Intentional Leadership requires a clear vision, defined values, and a willingness to take risks – but, more importantly, it requires a level of honesty with ourselves that comes from true awareness of who we are, what we stand for, and how we operate in life and business.

Anyone can access this level of awareness. It doesn't demand a spiritual or religious practice, or a guru, or even a big chunk of time. But it does require the willingness to look at how you're showing up in the moments that matter. It requires you to cultivate Unguarded Moments – quiet spaces where you can access a deeper level of knowledge, intuition, and clarity – and put what you learn there to work. And it requires you to be willing to change yourself in order to be better, do better, and *lead* better.

Self-awareness is crucial to leadership

Several years ago, while on a business trip to Florida, I took some time out to go scuba diving in Key West. I booked a dive trip, and early the next morning, 20 divers boarded the boat, all excited to see what the day had to offer. I was excited too – while we were still in the bay. But once we were out past the break wall, our 12m (40ft) powerboat was suddenly navigating 1.8m (6ft) waves. I'm an experienced diver with more than 1,000 dives under my belt, but I'm not a boat person.

After ten minutes or so on that rolling deck, I was pretty sure I was going to puke. As soon as we dropped anchor, I jumped into my gear and practically threw myself over the rail. But being in the water wasn't much better. I was still bobbing up and down like a cork, and now I was disoriented. I could barely keep track of the boat. The divemaster barked, 'Stay near the boat and hang on to the rope. We'll all go down together!' But I couldn't wait any longer, so down I went. Some 3–4.5m (10–15ft) below the waves, things were more settled. There was still a lot of back-and-forth motion from the surface, but the overwhelming nausea subsided a bit, and I was able to start to get my bearings.

Once everyone was in the water, we began the drift dive. We let the current carry us towards the reef and then dove much deeper, down to about 37m (120ft), into a canyon. Down there, the sun was like a distant spotlight, gently illuminating the coral and the canyon walls. The current was no longer a rushing force around me, but instead was a smooth undulation rocking me in the depths. I couldn't hear anything but my heartbeat, the hiss of my breath drawn through the regulator, or the *tap-tap* of parrotfish chomping the coral. It was profoundly peaceful. I felt, for the first time since beginning the dive, completely present, aware, trusting, empowered, connected, and completely without fear.

Later, back on the boat (where the waves had calmed a bit, thankfully), I reflected that life was a lot like this dive excursion. Most of us spend our time on the surface of our lives. As leaders, we're always trying to steer the boat and keep ourselves (and everyone else) afloat and organized. Every day, it's about survival – and we fear that, if we take our hands off the wheel, the next wave could swamp us. A few metres below the surface awaits our first experience of awareness. We can still feel the waves rolling above us, but they don't toss us around in quite the same way. At the same time, we are aware of the currents moving all around, and – if we're paying attention – get a glimpse of a whole new world that was invisible from the surface. We begin to sense how the entire picture comes together. But down deep is where the magic happens. It's where we can be still and *know*.

The deep space of inner stillness is where we will ultimately find the answers we spend so much of our 'surface time' seeking. Who are we? What matters to us? What drives our decisions? How can we do better, be better? How can we be Intentional Leaders, rather than reactionary managers? When we reach a certain depth, the stuff that doesn't matter falls away, and what's important reveals itself.

To step into a space of Intentional Leadership, we must do the deep dives, and do them often. We must find a place within ourselves where we can no longer be swayed by the surface currents or distracted by the waves. When we connect to who we are and what is non-negotiable, we will be able to recognize the deeper currents beneath the day-to-day of business and management. We will discover more Decisive and Defining Moments where we are being called to take a stand. We become more intentional in our leadership role, able to inspire and compel instead of directing and enforcing compliance.

Most people don't operate in this deep space in their everyday leadership. Either they don't think they have the time to make that space, or they don't understand why it's essential. As a result, they spend their lives on the surface of things, reacting to every swell, bailing out water, checking the weather, looking for the next thing to do – or, as in my case, just trying not to be sick all over everyone. Sometimes, they'll take a shallow dive to check things out, but soon they're back up there on the deck, fighting the fight of the moment.

Compel or comply?

I know many bad leaders who get good results – on paper. I'll bet you know a few as well. But let's face it: anyone can tell people what to do. It doesn't take talent, foresight, or sensitivity to be a hierarchical, top-down manager. And yet, so many people equate effective leadership with this classic command-and-control type of management.

What makes a good leader isn't the fact that people do what you say – because, let's face it, if they work for you, they pretty much have to. It's that they *want* to do what you ask, because they believe that you're a person who is worth listening to and following. Great leaders *compel* their teams to act, rather than expecting them to comply.

Today's workforce doesn't want command structures. They want autonomy. Input. Meaning. Purpose. They want to make an impact, not punch a clock. Creating and leading an empowered, purposeful workforce takes a new and different kind of leader – an Intentional Leader.

We've all heard the golden rule: 'Treat others as you would like to be treated.' This applies just as powerfully in leadership as it does in other types of relationships. If we want people to respect us, we need to freely extend them respect – even when our opinions and methods differ. If we want people to get excited about their work, we need to be excited about it too. If we want others to follow where we lead, we need to become the leaders that others can trust, respect, and admire enough to follow.

Before 9/11, I understood this theoretically. But it wasn't until I had to 'rally the troops' on 12 September 2001 that I understood it at a gut level. I couldn't let my own fear and uncertainty guide my actions. I had to show up for my team like never before – and, simultaneously, be willing to trust myself like never before.

Early in my career, I worked with several 'top-down' managers who desperately wanted trust but seldom extended it. I didn't want to replicate that behaviour. Trust wasn't easy for me; I grew up in a dysfunctional home where trust was a synonym for either weakness or stupidity. But at this critical time, I couldn't expect my team to just trust me because I was the boss – and I *definitely* couldn't leave everyone in the dark or let them try to process what had just happened on their own. I had to bring down some of my internal walls, show up fully, and set the example I wanted my employees and managers to follow. I had to be open, vulnerable, transparent, and respectful. And I had to stand by those values, *especially* when all I wanted to do was bury my head in work and pretend none of this crazy stuff was happening.

Many people use the terms 'leader' and 'manager' interchangeably. I certainly did, early in my career. But while effective managers can also be great leaders, the two are not the same. Both focus on creating results, but from different angles. Management is about goals, numbers, concrete metrics, and maintaining the status quo. Leadership is about driving improvement, building relationships, and uplifting people.

The best way to stop being managers and become leaders is to get to know ourselves at a deeper level – to dive beneath the surface of everyday tasks and challenges, and observe the deep currents at play. Actually, I'll go further than that. Inner growth and personal development are the best – and perhaps the only – tools we need to become true, Intentional Leaders. Everything else is secondary.

Most of us pay a lot of attention to our external selves. We know how tall we are, how much we weigh, how strong we are, how far we can run, how we look in the mirror. However, there is also an internal self with which many of us are less familiar. This inner self drives our Core Ideology, our self-value, our beliefs, our feelings – and above all, our 'why'.

However, whether we know it or not, our decisions are based on what's happening inside us – in the place of the deep currents. Until we can actually see and understand what transpires in that space, we will never be able to control or direct it. We will never be able to harness that power and use it to further our vision and inspire others.

One of the fundamental definitions of 'consciousness' is the mind becoming aware of itself. Humans are the only species (that we know of) that have *two* minds: the thinking mind and the observing mind. We have the ability to witness our thoughts and inner dialogues from an objective perspective. We can spend our entire lives without activating this singular skill – but once we do, there's no going back.

When we face external pressures, stresses, and challenges, we need balance between our inner and outer selves. We need to be aware of what's happening *inside* in order to successfully navigate and shore ourselves up against whatever is happening *outside*. If the external pressure gets too great, and our inner self isn't prepared to stand firm, we will get crushed.

Increasing our level of consciousness – or 'observer mind' – allows us to *respond* rather than *react*. We can stay in touch with the big picture, rise above our 'fight, flight, or freeze' reactions, and make aligned decisions even in moments of crisis. We can, as Gandhi said, 'Be the change we wish to see in the world', and compel others to do the same.

Intentional Leaders lead from within

There's a growing gap between status quo leadership and Intentional Leadership, and it widens every time we take an action that is out of alignment with who we want to be and what we want to create in the world.

Some would say that the issue with leadership today is that there are so many 'bad guys' doing self-serving and malicious things. It seems like, every day, news outlets are sharing some new outrageousness perpetrated by this or that CEO or politician. But to me, the real crisis in modern leadership isn't that there are tyrants and crooks in power. There will always be tyrants and crooks, and they will always pursue their self-interest with no regard for consequences. No, the issue is that so many of the leaders surrounding these tyrants sit on their hands when they should be taking a stand for the values they claim to embody. They let the ends justify the means, and compromise their integrity in the process.

Even in organizations where tyrants don't rule, status quo leadership makes decisions that seem expedient in the now, but don't reflect a purposeful, values-driven, long-term vision. Like the boat bobbing on the surface of the ocean, this method of leadership fights the immediate problems without understanding or taking a stance on deeper issues, leaving everyone in the organization feeling lost, disconnected, undervalued, and uninspired.

In this book, I will teach you how to become an Intentional Leader. It's an inside-out journey into your own genius. It won't always be easy or comfortable – but I can promise you that, when you undertake it, it will be one of the most rewarding paths you have ever walked.

However, before we can take our first steps towards this goal, we need to tackle the biggest obstacle to aligned leadership that exists in our modern world – the surface-level space of wave-battling reactivity I call 'Ghost Mode'.

Turn the page, because it's time for a wake-up call.

Reflection

At the end of each chapter of this book, you'll find a short 'Reflection' section with recaps of several key points. These aren't intended to be Cliff Notes or shortcuts, but rather reminders to spur your thoughts about what you've learned. (They're also great for sharing on social media to start conversations with your network!)

- The real reason why leadership fails in so many organizations isn't a lack of resources, or a poorly trained team, or the economy, or any other external factor. Leadership fails *from the inside out* due to a lack of presence and self-awareness.
- Intentional Leadership requires a clear vision, defined values, and a willingness to take risks – but, more importantly, it requires a level of honesty with ourselves that comes from true awareness of who we are, what we stand for, and how we operate in life and business.
- Great leaders *compel* others to act, rather than simply expecting compliance.
- When we connect to who we are and what is non-negotiable, we will be able to recognize the deeper currents beneath the day-to-day of business and management. We will discover more Decisive and Defining Moments where we are being called to take a stand. We become more intentional in our leadership role, able to inspire and compel instead of directing and enforcing compliance.

Unity of Thought and Action

At Atrion, we had a maxim in leadership: 'Unity of Thought and Action', or UTA for short. This was a way for us to check in and make sure that there was no dissonance between what we talked about and what we took action around.

The best way to move beyond theoretical knowledge into actual evolution is to put what you've learned into practice. It's all well and good to understand something cognitively, but if you're not walking your talk, it's ultimately meaningless. That's why you'll find a UTA section at the end of every chapter in this book.

Thought – Intentional Leadership originates within us

Intentional Leadership isn't a task, or a protocol. It's a skillset that is created and refined through self-awareness and the willingness to learn and grow as people and as leaders.

How have you observed this in your own leadership journey?

Action – go below the surface

Reflect on previous Unguarded Moments and how they have impacted you. Then, make a plan to create space for quiet reflection or meditation this week – to go beneath the surface and look at what is happening there.

During your Unguarded Moment, remember a leadership moment that felt powerful or profound to you. What was happening in your inner world during that moment, and how did it translate into your outer experience?

CHAPTER 2

Ghost Mode: The Antithesis of Intentional Leadership

'As long as a man stands in his own way, everything seems to be in his way.' – Emerson

I once consulted for a company where the CEO was in full-on Ghost Mode. George was a very busy guy, and very conscious of all the important stuff he had to do. When he wasn't at his desk, he had his nose to his phone, checking off task after task from his list. In short, he was exactly what we've been trained to expect in an executive.

Every day, George walked by the desk of his receptionist, Anna, on his way into his office. He didn't nod or say hello. He didn't ask her how her day was. Anna was doing her job, and he was doing his, and – in his mind, at least – that was as it should be.

When I come into a new company as a consultant, I make it a priority to get to know the staff – even those who aren't directly involved in my programme. Knowing who they are and what they value gives me a sense of what the company is all about, and where we need to focus on helping leadership 'level up'.

From the start, it was clear that Anna was demoralized. One day, after I'd said good morning and asked after her kids, she confided, 'I wish our CEO cared as much about my day as you do. I feel like I don't even exist most of the time!'

I'd seen it too. George was an effective manager, and he was great with numbers, but he was always thinking three steps ahead. He never stopped to consider how his habit of living in his head impacted his employees. We had numerous conversations about this, and at one point, he even acknowledged that he was falling short in his work relationships – but his actions never changed.

After it became clear that George wasn't going to take the initiative, I made it a point to spend time with Anna whenever I was there. She was exceptional at her job. Clients loved her warm manner and efficiency. And when, one day, I was doing a last-minute presentation for the sales team and hadn't made it to the printer to get my worksheets, she dropped everything to make it happen for me. I sent her a little desk ornament in gratitude, which she displayed proudly. CEO George never noticed the addition to her desk. But he *did* notice when she put in her resignation three weeks later.

'I don't get it!' he confided. 'I paid her well. She had great benefits. The salespeople all liked her. Why would she just up and leave?'

That's Ghost Mode in action.

Ghost Mode is the polar opposite of Intentional Leadership – the result of a systemic lack of awareness. Unfortunately, it's also the modus operandi for leadership at every level, in companies around the world. In some companies, it's the way leadership is *expected* to behave.

Here's a hard truth about leadership. The people you're leading don't judge you by what's going on in your head (because they can't see that) or by how good you look on paper. They judge you by your *actions* – particularly by your actions towards them personally. (Remember the golden rule?) And regardless of how well you think you hide it, the people around you will always know when you're operating in Ghost Mode, and they will respond accordingly.

When we're operating on the surface level, always looking towards the next milestone or crisis, it's hard to be present to what's happening in the moment, especially if it doesn't appear to impact our job directly, our numbers, or our sense of place in our organization. We pass right by Defining Moments without ever noticing them, like ghosts walking through a crowded hallway.

George wasn't an uncaring guy. He wasn't a jerk. But he *was* in full-on Ghost Mode. His attention was always on the future or the past, never on the now. His relationship with Anna didn't appear, on the surface, to impact the results he was chasing … but in the end, it did, in a big way. His lack of presence – his lack of Intentional Leadership – cost him one of his most engaged and dedicated front-line employees.

There are currents moving through your team, your department, and your organization. Sometimes these are currents of optimism and excitement. Other times, they're currents of fear, uncertainty, or discontent.

As a leader, *you* are one of the primary forces driving those currents. Who you are, what you stand for, what you acknowledge or ignore, what you say and what you don't: all these things matter. The deep currents of your organization flow from you – *whether you realize it or not.*

The currents you create don't stop at your office door, either. They flow through every aspect of your life. You can't be one person at home and another on the job. When you try to do that, you're just hopping on a different boat, not redirecting the water underneath.

If you want to be a true leader, make time in Unguarded Moments to go below the chaos. Get to know who you are and what you stand for as a person and a leader. Only then can you have the clarity, conviction, and insight to put your attention where it matters, when it matters.

When you do this, you *create* the currents, instead of battling them.

What is Ghost Mode?

Chances are, you know Ghost Mode when you see it…in other people. You probably recognized an old (or current) boss in the story I just shared about George and Anna. You probably have been on the receiving end of someone else's version of captaining the boat at surface level. You have probably been confused by someone who claims to uphold a particular set of values but often fails to act according to those values. You have probably felt a disconnect between leadership and the rest of the company.

But what you may not realize is that you, too, may be in Ghost Mode in one or more aspects of your day-to-day work. In fact, if you're feeling like your current leadership journey isn't taking you and your team where you want to go, it's very likely that there's some aspect of Ghost Mode at play.

Ghost Mode, simply defined, is the polar opposite of Intentional Leadership. It's not only the lack of presence, understanding, or awareness – that's just how it shows up on the surface. In fact, Ghost Mode is a disconnected state of being that presents as four distinct 'symptoms'.

The four symptoms of Ghost Mode:

1 Lack of presence
2 Lack of trust/reactionism
3 Unhealthy ego
4 Disconnection

All of these symptoms are expressed uniquely from person to person, but they're easy to recognize when you know what to look for. Most of us regularly slip into an expression of one or more of these symptoms. They're our surface-level comfort zones; the behaviours we default to when we're not paying attention.

Ghost Mode perpetuates itself. Unconsciously (or even consciously), we make excuses for being in this mode. Maybe we have a sense that there's something else we should be doing, some different way of approaching our daily tasks and relationships. Still, instead of changing our behaviours, we find ourselves listing all of the perfectly valid reasons for our actions. They make sense to us because we're absorbed in fighting the waves of the moment.

If this hits a nerve for you, it's OK. We all slip into Ghost Mode sometimes. But once you become aware of what's happening, you can cultivate awareness, practise presence, and make different choices. This is where the journey of Intentional Leadership begins.

As you can see in the chart below, there are antidotes to the four symptoms of Ghost Mode. These are the Four Pillars of the Intentional Leadership model.

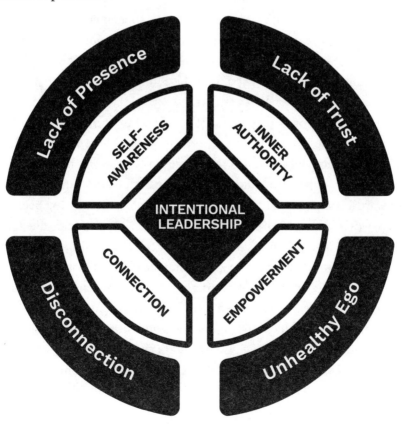

In the following sections, we'll break down the symptoms of Ghost Mode one by one, and learn how greater presence and awareness can bring us out of Ghost Mode and into Intentional Leadership.

Ghost Mode symptom 1: lack of presence

This is precisely what I described in my story about scuba diving in Chapter 1. When we're too wrapped up in problem-solving, troubleshooting, living in the future (or the past), and putting out fires, we forget to show up for what really matters – namely, opportunities, relationships, and Decisive Moments. We're on autopilot; our bodies are going through the motions, but our brains are operating three days ahead. Consequently, we miss a lot of the detail, depth, and meaning around what's happening in the *now*.

Lack of presence is walking by your receptionist's desk every day without noticing anything except that she got there on time. It's missing cues from your team that they need guidance and moral support, not just metrics and ultimatums. It's ploughing doggedly through your presentation when it's clear that half the room is falling asleep and the other half is looking at their watches.

It's also checking a text message or glancing at your smartwatch when your employee is visibly upset, or when you're in the middle of a crucial conversation. It's that time you blew off the new sales guy because he had no clout, but now he's your boss (and isn't *that* awkward). It's spacing out during an important client meeting because you're worried about getting the deal and your mind is racing ahead to the contract negotiation. It's driving by an accident scene and thinking, 'I have to get to work – but I'm sure someone else will stop to help.'

For me, lack of presence is tuning out my wife when she speaks to me over dinner because my head is so full from the day that I can't turn off my thoughts. It's like missing the beautiful scenery on a mountain hike because my head is back home with a client. It's closing my office door when I know my team needs me to leave it open. There's always an excuse – but that doesn't make the behaviour excusable.

Presence is about showing up fully for yourself and the people around you. However, it's not just about gaining the ability to read social cues effectively. Presence confers *the ability to determine what is happening in the moment and respond accordingly.* In other words, it helps you harness the power of those Decisive Moments that would otherwise skate by unnoticed.

The antidote to lack of presence is *self-awareness.* The more we get to know ourselves – particularly, who we are, what we value, and what we stand for in the world – the more we can show up for ourselves and others in a way that feels congruent, intentional, and aligned.

We'll take a much closer look at this in Chapter 3, but for now, I want you to ask yourself: 'Where do I struggle to stay present?'

Just asking that question will have profound effects on your level of awareness.

Ghost Mode symptom 2: lack of trust/reactionism

'You just need to trust me.'

I can't count the number of times I heard bosses and managers say that throughout my early career. And, paradoxically, it always came out of the mouths of people I didn't trust, and who didn't seem inclined to trust me.

Many of us learned, early on, that trust is a commodity. In order to give it, we need to receive it. The question then becomes: who starts that process? Who extends the hand first?

Lack of trust is a primary indicator that someone is in Ghost Mode. Instead of going deep, looking at the currents, and making choices deliberately about how, when, and why to extend trust, Ghost Mode assumes that trust happens somewhere outside of this moment, according to some ephemeral set of criteria. It's just another manifestation of a lack of presence.

Interestingly, for many (if not most) of my coaching and training clients, trust is one of their biggest challenges. They point to incidents from the past as reasons why they can't trust their employees, their bosses, their partners. But most of all, they talk about how they don't fully trust themselves to make the right decisions in Decisive Moments. So, they take no action at all – which is an action in itself – and the choices are made for them.

In order to trust ourselves as Intentional Leaders, we need a strong *Core Ideology* – a trifecta of clear and well-defined values, purpose, and vision. This provides a framework for our day-to-day decision-making and helps us stay consistent in challenging situations. Moreover, it provides a pathway for others to connect with us on a personal level and extend their trust to us.

Trust, like leadership, is an inside-out process. I'll show you how to create and define your powerful Core Ideology in Chapter 4 – but for now, I invite you to consider that the process of becoming self-aware leads inevitably to greater *inner authority*, which is the only real antidote to lack of trust in yourself and others.

Emerson's words about the 'iron string' from the Introduction impacted my teenage self so strongly because I didn't trust myself (or anyone else, for that matter). I was looking, in some way, for the certainty of my inner authority. It took me a while longer to find it – but that journey changed everything.

To begin your own dialogue around this concept, ask, 'Do I trust myself?' If so, why? And if not, why not?

Ghost Mode symptom 3: unhealthy ego

If you've done any kind of self-exploration, spiritual practice, or even conventional talk therapy, you'll know that ego gets a bad rap in many circles.

We all have an ego. It's part of our human construction. It helps us identify as individual beings and separate our stories and experiences from those of other people. It helps us retain our autonomy and inner authority. Like any other tool, the ego can be helpful to us if we use it correctly. It can facilitate balance between our inner experience and our outer world. It can help us stay true to our Core Ideology and navigate relationships with integrity. But, like any other tool, it becomes a liability and a weakness if overused, underused, or misused.

Visualize ego as a stereo dial with a range from zero to 10.

If I've got the dial fixed at a two, I can't hear my inner voice over all the noise around me. I get caught up in other people's soundtracks or overwhelmed by the critical voices in my head. Some people call this 'inferior ego' or 'people pleasing'.

On the other hand, if I have the volume turned up to nine, I can't hear anything other than my own soundtrack. People talk to me, but their words don't land; I can't hear others' experiences or ideas. You might call this range 'big head syndrome'; in the extreme, it looks like egocentricity and narcissism.

It's as unhealthy for a leader to be at the 'low' end of the ego spectrum as at the high end. Both are manifestations of Ghost Mode. Both create an imbalance between our inner and outer worlds, undermine trust and self-awareness, and create a sense of disconnection from others.

When we are operating too far to either side of the ego continuum, we disconnect from real-time situations and relationships. We become wrapped up in ourselves – our perceived superiority or inferiority, our dramas, our unmet needs. We can't engage fully with what's happening around us. We can't hold healthy boundaries for ourselves and others. Our decisions are not based in our beliefs, principles, vision, or team's needs; rather, they are a conditioned reaction to whatever story our ego is telling us. It's like we're in a cinema with a group of other people, but instead of watching the big screen, we're watching a completely different movie on our iPad.

The antidote to an unhealthy or unbalanced ego is *empowerment* of self and others. The ability to truly let others shine is one of the characteristics all great leaders share – and yet, few people know how to create it.

The ability to empower is built on the foundation of self-awareness and inner authority. The best relationships happen when we have a balance between the soundtrack in our head and our ability to hear, see, and acknowledge others. From this middle ground, we see ourselves and each other more clearly, harness our complementary strengths, and create momentum.

We will explore the concept of empowerment further in Chapter 5, but for now, ask yourself, 'Where on the dial is my ego right now?'

Ghost Mode symptom 4: disconnection

A few moments in my life stand out as profound moments of connection. The first time I stood at the rim of the Grand Canyon and realized how *big* the world was. My mentee's graduation ceremony, at which she began her Valedictorian speech with the words, 'I was born addicted to crack cocaine.' Standing in front of my team on 12 September 2001, and watching the fear and hope in their faces as the world shifted under our feet.

Have you ever felt like you were a part of something bigger than yourself? How amazingly supported, purposeful, and fulfilled did you feel in those moments?

And have you ever felt like you showed up every day for a person or organization that didn't care about you at all? Like you were just a cog in a giant machine, churning out results that were ultimately meaningless?

One is an example of Intentional Leadership in action. The other is Ghost Mode.

When leadership is in Ghost Mode, they are disconnected – from individuals, from their teams, from their mission, and from the greater purpose of the work they're doing. Instead of focusing on relationships, they're focused on results. Instead of focusing on people, they're focused on numbers, metrics, and tangible short-term goals. They're always living three steps ahead of where they are. They're untethered, like real ghosts. And their lack of presence causes everyone around them to disconnect as well. In essence, leaders in Ghost Mode create teams of Ghosts.

Great leaders have the power to connect everyone around them to something greater than themselves – to a vision, a goal, or a unifying cause. But to be that kind of leader, we first need to know who we are and what we stand for … and then, we need to find a way to express our Core Ideology in a way everyone can understand and hold themselves accountable to. This, more than anything else, helps the people on our teams feel like they belong and can contribute.

Connection is possibly the most challenging pillar of Intentional Leadership because it's the least definable. It goes far beyond simply looking someone in the eyes or acknowledging their presence. Connection looks different for everyone; there is no formula or silver bullet. But, as they say, 'You'll know it when you see it' – and you'll know it when you don't.

Building true connection in your relationships is next to impossible until you know yourself and trust in your inner authority. However, once you've built that internal foundation, your connections will become unique, authentic, transformational, and enduring.

We'll talk more about connection in Chapter 6, but for now, ask yourself, 'Am I truly creating and experiencing connection as a leader?'

Unguarded Moments support Intentional Leadership

I defined Unguarded Moments in the Introduction as 'the moments of inner clarity and stillness where our authentic self manifests in a natural and uncontrolled manner'. Sometimes, these moments happen spontaneously – often when we're doing something that brings us joy. They happen when we're in nature and suddenly forget about everything except the majesty right in front of us. They happen to musicians and artists as a sort of creative trance, where time is suspended and inspiration comes through in a flood. They happen to people in love. They happen to scientists engrossed in a problem. When these moments come, they're viewed as miracles, gifts from the Muses, or divine inspiration.

Unguarded Moments can be all of those things, but I think of them differently. I see them as *flashes of alignment* where, instead of a cluttered, winding street full of obstacles, we have a direct and unobstructed line of sight to who we truly are – and who we truly are has a direct line of access to us.

The Four Pillars of Intentional Leadership are the antidotes to Ghost Mode, but Unguarded Moments are the key to unlocking the power of those Pillars. You will create Unguarded Moments in your own way; it's something you will learn with practice. What I will teach you in this book is how to use the information you receive from those moments in a way that actually moves you forwards as a leader.

The first step, of course, is awareness.

If you've been in some aspect of Ghost Mode for your whole career, don't beat yourself up about it. You didn't intentionally put yourself there. There was no one day when you woke up and said, 'Forget this whole presence thing. I'm going Ghost.' But now that you know where you are and what you're up against, you can make different choices. You can come back to life, and step into your role as a leader in a way you never have before.

* * *

Right now, you may be thinking, 'What the heck did I get myself into? I didn't think this was a book about inner-truth-spiritual-crap. I picked this up to learn about *leadership*!' And I'm here to tell you, there is no better way to become a *true* leader – the kind of leader whom people want to follow – than to know who you are and lead from that place. No one wants to follow a ghost.

You've reached a Decisive Moment. Right now, you need to choose whether you are willing and excited to have a new conversation about Intentional Leadership, and to approach your identity as a leader from a new perspective. If you want to become the kind of leader who inspires and invites rather than disciplines and demands – the kind of leader who stands for more than just the bottom line – then read on, my friend.

As Emerson said: 'This time, like all times, is a very good one, if we but know what to do with it.'

Reflection

- Intentional Leadership is a choice. We *choose* to lead. We choose how and when we show up for others. We choose to bring our best selves forwards. However, sometimes we slip into Ghost Mode. Ghost Mode is the polar opposite of Intentional Leadership.

- Ghost Mode is not the lack of presence, understanding, or awareness – that's just how it shows up on the surface. In fact, it is more like a cancer sitting below the surface of our awareness, affecting every leadership decision we make. Ghost Mode is a disconnected state of being that presents as four distinct 'symptoms': lack of presence, lack of trust/reactionism, unhealthy ego, and disconnection.

- Becoming an Intentional Leader requires our complicity. We choose how and when we show up. The Four Pillars of Intentional Leadership are the antidotes to Ghost Mode. They are: self-awareness, inner authority, empowerment, and connection.

- Unguarded Moments are the keys to unlocking the Four Pillars of Intentional Leadership. Occasionally, we must shift from our thinking, tactical, and reacting world to something that creates space for observation, long-term thinking, and creating powerful response mechanisms.

Unity of Thought and Action

Thought – begin to cultivate awareness

We are a combination of good and weak leadership traits and behaviours. Sometimes we slip into Ghost Mode and fail to show up appropriately. By creating space to cultivate the Unguarded Moment, we can examine our beliefs, actions, and behaviours objectively, using our observing mind. This allows us to create pathways for positive change. As they say, when you know better, you do better.

Action – create Unguarded Moments

The first step to inviting greater intentionality in leadership is to create space to reflect upon your leadership role and how you perform. Create a daily routine that allows you windows of 10–15 minutes of quiet time for that purpose. Use your calendar tool to schedule time for your Unguarded Moments practice. (Placing this critical time on your calendar protects this space.)

One great way to start your Unguarded Moment practice is to take three to five deep breaths. Breathe in through your nose while slowly counting to four. Hold your breath for a few seconds once your lungs are full, then exhale through your mouth while slowly counting to eight. Deep breathing helps you create inner calmness and sink beneath the tumultuous waves of life. Once you feel calm, contemplate one or more of the following questions.

- What are some of the strong leadership traits that you possess?
- What moments are most likely to bring out the best version of yourself?
- Where are you experiencing one or more symptoms of Ghost Mode?
- Where do you recognize Ghost Mode in others around you?
- How has the presence of Ghost Mode in yourself and others affected your experience in work and leadership?

Part II

CHAPTER 3

Self-awareness: Your Leadership Superpower

'We do not yet possess ourselves, and we know at the same time that we are much more.' – Emerson

I grew up in a very dysfunctional household. My mother was an alcoholic. My dad ... let's just say he had anger issues. I got the crap beaten out of me regularly, and after I was about four, my mother no longer put herself in the middle of those showdowns.

However, even with all this going on, I realized that I wasn't the problem. The people around me were doing bad things, but that wasn't because *I* was bad – it was because they didn't know any better. This knowing was probably the only thing that kept me functional. It kept me sober and mostly sane. But it also made me very, very angry. I had a chip on my shoulder the size of Mount Everest, and a deep sensitivity to injustice.

As a teenager, I loved to fight. I would seize any opportunity to engage in an altercation. The opportunities I loved the most was when I got to fight someone who was bullying a smaller kid. It was like being Batman. My desire to get better at fighting led me to martial arts. I started taking Judo classes at a local studio when I was 16.

Six months into my studies, my fighting skills had improved significantly. I was invited to compete in a small tournament with a dojo across town. I went there with my head held high, confident with my newly acquired skills, and...well, I kicked ass.

It didn't matter to me whether the other kids were bigger or smaller than me, or how many belt levels they'd earned. I was in it to win it.

As you can imagine, my head swelled to the size of a football field after this. I started fighting more in school, talking trash, and terrorizing any bully who dared show his face in the yard.

Then, one day, I showed up for Judo class to find the place empty except for my sensei and his wife, a petite woman named Norah who looked like she weighed all of 90 pounds. My sensei said, 'Tim, we can do one of two things. We can all head home, or you can work with my wife. She's training for her brown belt test, and she needs a sparring partner.'

'I'm in,' I said.

I don't think I stood up straight for more than three seconds at a time for the next two hours. That tiny woman threw me from one end of the dojo to the other. She never said a word. Every time she knocked me down, I got more and more frustrated and aggressive – but the more I tried to channel that aggression into our sparring, the faster she knocked me down.

When it was over, I sat there on my butt for a few minutes, totally stunned. I had just had my ass kicked by a woman half my size who was old enough to be my mother. Without a word, I gathered up my stuff and did my walk of shame to the front door. Before I could leave, though, my sensei came up and put his hand on my shoulder.

'In life, there's always someone better than you. Remember that.'

Five minutes later, chewing on my sore lip, I suddenly had a realization. I slammed on the brakes, pulled over to the side of the road, and pounded the steering wheel with my fist.

'Son of a bitch! He set that up!'

It was painfully obvious in hindsight: my sensei and his wife had orchestrated the whole encounter to teach me a lesson.

It was a pure Unguarded Moment. It was like the road forked in front of me. I was simultaneously furious and awestruck. My thoughts went silent. I had been presented with an opportunity, and I had to make a choice. I could accept this lesson and try to learn from it, or I could retreat into my fury and make this just another example of how people were jerks, and everyone was out to get me.

I still don't know why I chose the former. But the minute I decided to learn what my sensei had been trying to teach me, I had one of the most profound epiphanies of my life. I was 'fighting the good fight'. I was using my brawling skills to defend those who couldn't protect themselves. And yet, by beating up those bullies, I was becoming exactly the kind of person I had sworn to myself I would never be – a person who hurt other people just because I could. I was fighting back at my father, and becoming just like him, at the same time.

There would always be someone better than me. So if I wanted to break out of the pattern of violence in which I'd lived for my entire 16 years of life, I had to find a better way to solve my problems and feel good about myself – because otherwise, the fights would never stop.

From that day on, I stopped looking for fights. I used words and humour to defuse situations instead. And I found that my peers respected me more than when I'd been the king of fistfights.

My sensei and I never spoke about that night, but I never forgot how he and his wife took that time to invest in me. Whether they were fully aware of it or not, it was a Defining Moment for them. They literally changed the course of my life.

Turning the lens inwards

Sometimes, awareness comes to us all wrapped up in a nice package, and sometimes it comes as a punch in the face. It's not our job to decide how we learn. It's our job to *decide to learn when the opportunity presents itself*. The only way we can recognize and be open to the lessons life has to teach us is by looking inwards and cultivating awareness.

What does this have to do with leadership, you ask? *Everything.*

Before we can ask others to follow us, we first need to understand who we are, what we value, and what we are striving to create. And the only way to do that is to *start paying attention*.

Numerous studies have shown that presence – the act of paying attention, otherwise known as mindfulness – has been shown to increase happiness, decrease stress, and create better relationships. It measurably improves focus, cognition, and execution. But most importantly, presence invites and perpetuates self-awareness, which is the first and most crucial step to emerging from Ghost Mode into Intentional Leadership.

We can't navigate effectively in our outer world if we are blind to what shapes our inner world. That's why, as leaders, we need to make it a priority to learn who we are, inside and out. We need to witness ourselves operating in the spaces we occupy. And we need to understand that, while we can't control every circumstance, our inner 'default' isn't the best – or only – option available to us.

When we live and lead with a lack of presence and awareness, we are in Ghost Mode. We are reacting to people, situations, and things. We are in a perpetual 'firefighting' mode. We might even feel like everyone and everything is against us. Because we can't see our actions and reactions as part of the equation that creates our situation, we might blame other people, our company, the economy, the market, technology, etc. for the issues we experience. Or we might take all the blame on ourselves and end up paralyzed with fear and self-doubt. And while we might achieve 'success' in this state, we will never achieve greatness as leaders.

Turning our focus inwards is the first step towards Intentional Leadership because it takes us out of that reactionary space. It allows us to see ourselves more clearly and examine *why* we do what we do. It invites us to engage with each experience as a learning moment, and opens the door for us to think, behave, and engage with others in new, more productive ways.

And when we come to a place where our road forks – a Decisive or Defining Moment – it helps us choose our path with precise and deliberate intention.

Cognitive dissonance and Ghost Mode

Before that pivotal evening with my sensei and his wife, I was deep in Ghost Mode. I mean, those bullies were *asking* to be beaten up. I wasn't starting the fights, only finishing them. I was the good guy – a vigilante, like Batman. I had a thousand ways of justifying my actions to myself. Some of them were even valid.

And yet, part of me knew that my behaviour wasn't congruent with who I wanted to be and the kind of life I wanted to create. It wasn't a conscious thought so much as a feeling of uneasiness that was always boiling in my gut. Even though I was winning my fights, I had a sense of shame about my actions. I'd always pushed that shame aside with righteous anger ... but now, I saw that every time I did that, I lost a part of myself.

I know now that what I was experiencing was *cognitive dissonance*, a psychological state in which our beliefs and actions are in opposition to one another.

In music, 'dissonance' is used to describe two or more tones that are not in harmony with one another. Dissonance creates tension that needs to be resolved. In musical works, tension is used as a tool to draw the listener in and create heightened emotion – but in the end, it must be resolved into consonance (harmony); otherwise, the piece feels incomplete.

When we are simultaneously trying to maintain two opposing beliefs or ideas, it creates a similar dissonance in our minds – a state of uncertainty, discomfort, tension, anxiety, stress, and instability. But the more we try to justify or push away this dissonance, the further we get from being authentic.

We all live with cognitive dissonance to some degree or another. We promise ourselves that we'll get healthy, then gorge on Doritos and ice cream. We talk about increasing productivity while wasting hours a day on social media and email. We want to be great leaders, but we're too intimidated to take a stand when conflict arises. We want others to trust us, but we trust no one. Cognitive dissonance is a key factor in Ghost Mode – and it's the direct result of lack of awareness. How we deal with it will determine how we grow and succeed as Intentional Leaders.

My belief that I was 'fighting the good fight' in the playground and my certainty that I didn't want to be a violent man like my father were in opposition. I couldn't occupy both spaces at once. I couldn't be violent and non-violent at the same time. When this was shown to me through my experience with my sensei, I had two choices: I could justify my actions and continue my cognitive dissonance, or I could stop, look within, and choose the path that led me towards what I really wanted – a resolution of my inner dissonance and conflict – even if I didn't like what that path showed me about myself.

The thing is, cognitive dissonance is a gift. It draws our attention to an area where growth is needed. However, most of us don't see inner tension this way. Instead, we see it as a clue that someone or something is trying to make us 'wrong'.

In his research, renowned political scientist Drew Westen found that reasoning virtually shuts down when we are confronted with information dissonant to our beliefs. In one study, conducted during the US Presidential election in 2004, adherents to both major political parties were confronted with 'threatening' information about their candidate. fMRI monitoring showed what parts of their brains were engaged during this exercise. None of the 'reasoning' circuits lit up. Instead, circuits for emotional management and conflict resolution were engaged. More, once the participants had 'resolved' the issue – meaning, they found ways to deflect or ignore the information that distressed them, as not one person reported having changed their opinion – their brains switched off the negative emotions associated with feeling challenged, and activated neurocircuitry related to reward.

When we perceive someone is trying to make us wrong, we go into a cycle of self-defending, in which we explain to ourselves over and over why we did what we did, and what our actions mean about us. We rationalize every step we took within the situation. We tell ourselves we were right, and others wrong. Conversely, we make *ourselves* wrong, and use that story to fuel our feelings of inferiority. In the end, both angles are self-justifying; neither serves us or our goals.

To lead intentionally, we need to stop making ourselves right at all costs. Self-justifying behaviour doesn't resolve the dissonance we feel; it amplifies it. Deep down, on a subconscious level, we know that our choices are creating the dissonance in the first place. We need to dive below our surface-level feelings to figure out what's driving our actions, and change the direction of that deep current to create different results.

The antidote to cognitive dissonance is self-awareness. Instead of walking around on autopilot, doing things the way we've always done them (and then justifying those things the way we've always justified them), we can train ourselves to pause, observe, and acknowledge what's really going on. What do we think? How do we feel? How do we react? And, most importantly: are those thoughts, feelings, and reactions the only options available to us?

Where does the road fork? And what would we learn if we took the road we haven't travelled before?

Five Steps to Grow Your Self-awareness

At this point, you probably have a sense of why self-awareness is an essential tool for Intentional Leadership. But if you've never engaged with a practice like this before, it can be challenging to know where to start.

By reflecting on my own leadership journey, and those of the hundreds of leaders I've had the privilege to coach and mentor, I've concluded that self-awareness is an ongoing, multi-step process.

The five steps to grow your self-awareness are:

1. Create space through Unguarded Moments.
2. Connect to your inner world.
3. Collect objective information.
4. Assess your goals.
5. Ask for feedback.

At any point in time, we should be engaged with at least one of these steps. When you've had some practice, you'll learn to flow through them all on a daily basis and stay in a constant feedback loop of observation, assimilation, and reflection. This is an optimal state for growth ... and it starts with the creation of Unguarded Moments.

Step 1: create space through Unguarded Moments

The Unguarded Moment is the most powerful tool at your disposal to invite self-observation and self-awareness. As we learned in Chapter 1, Unguarded Moments are moments when you drop all the masks, pretences, and expectations, and allow your true self to come to the forefront. They're moments when you're completely authentic and without pretence – and therefore open to creativity, truth, innovation, and personal growth.

When I speak about the concept of Unguarded Moments, the first thing most people ask is how to create them.

My reply? 'It's less about *how* you do it, and more about your intention.'

For example, have you ever been out for a run, and suddenly a brilliant idea or realization strikes you seemingly out of nowhere? You might even find yourself stopping at the side of the road so you can process this incredible piece of awareness. Or, have you ever been sitting in meditation and simply *known* the answer to the question you were asking? Or, have you ever told a trusted friend about a problem, then listened to the solution fall out of your mouth before you've even finished the question?

All of these are examples of Unguarded Moments. When you put yourself in a space where you can *get out of your own way*, you will become open enough to receive the knowledge that already exists within you.

I create Unguarded Moments through meditation, hiking, running, yoga, and conversation with friends and mentors I trust. Each of these activities tunes my focus differently, but the results are always the same: I learn something about myself, and that knowledge helps me see a better way forwards.

Right about now, you're probably saying, 'This is great, but when the heck am I going to have time for this?' Here's the hard truth: you have to *create* the time. You make it a priority. You must jump off the rocking boat and let yourself dive deep.

When you create Unguarded Moments, you turn off your Ghost Mode switch. Doing this daily, or even just a few times a week, can make a huge difference in how you show up in your role as a leader.

When you start playing with Unguarded Moments, tools like guided meditations or music can help you get into a quiet head space. Walking in nature (without your devices!) is also a great way to dive in. Journaling with specific prompts is another. But no matter how you choose to structure this time, the one thing you absolutely must be is *present*. If you find your thoughts wandering, or your mind starts to tell stories, just come back to the here and now. Find something in this moment to focus on – whether it's your breath, the voice on the recorded meditation, the wind in the trees, or something else. And remember that, just like anything else, creating Unguarded Moments takes practice.

Step 2: connect to your inner world

The best way to get to know yourself is simply to *be* with yourself absent any distractions. It's a bit like starting a new dating relationship. At first, things can be awkward. You might be fidgety and act weird as you look for something that resonates between you and the other person. Then, as the relationship grows, everything gets more comfortable. You start to talk about the deeper stuff. You get a glimpse of real truth.

Self-awareness is like that. At first, sitting with yourself in a quiet space with nothing to look at, touch, or talk to will make you want to climb out of your skin. But soon, it will get more comfortable. You'll begin to observe the conversations that go on in your head. You'll get to know what makes you tick.

If this all sounds a bit...crazy, don't panic. It's the way our human brains are designed. We have a thinking mind, and we have a consciousness or higher mind – the observing mind. This split cognition is why we can identify our thoughts as 'things that we think' and not as indisputable pieces of reality. We are the only creatures on the planet (that we know of) who can step outside our thoughts and feelings, observe them, and change them through choice.

Eastern traditions do an outstanding job of explaining this; if you're curious, I recommend reading Taoist, Buddhist, or Yogic philosophy. If that doesn't resonate, don't worry. It's enough to know that you have two aspects of 'you' operating simultaneously: one that is automatic and unconscious, and another that has the capacity to observe, intervene with, and redirect the first.

In a sense, connecting to your inner world is really about getting to know yourself from the perspective of this 'other' you – the observing mind – and allowing that part of you to have more of a say on a day-to-day basis.

Let's just say that there's far more to you than you may have realized – and it's going to be a really interesting ride.

Step 3: collect objective information

In addition to regularly creating Unguarded Moments and connecting to their inner worlds, I often recommend that my clients and students engage with tools that will give them objective, impersonal information about who they are, what they do, and why they do it.

Some great sources of objective information are personal assessment tools. These tools allow us to gain additional perspective on ourselves, our values, and our motivations. More importantly, they give us a language to use to accelerate self-awareness.

One or more of these tools are probably familiar to you; you may have already used them personally or with your team. However, the way I look at these tools might be different from what you're used to.

Too many people take assessments at face value; they make them the holy grail of self-awareness, and let their results dictate what is and isn't possible for them as leaders. They say, 'This says I'm good at X, but I stink at Y, so I guess [insert desired result here] isn't on the cards for me.' This is precisely the *wrong* way to use self-assessments.

I think of assessments as maps of our internal landscape. They show us our ideal route to get to the desired end point, and where we might need to pay extra attention to the terrain. But they don't dictate where we can go, and where we can't. Maps are impartial and objective.

In my view, we all have superpowers, and we all have learning curves. There is no right or wrong, no good or bad, when it comes to who we are. We simply need to understand the raw materials of us so we can use our natural talents to their greatest potential. Or, as the famous Renaissance painter Michelangelo once said, 'Every block of stone has a statue inside it and it is the task of the sculptor to discover it.'

A few self-assessment tools stand out to me as being particularly helpful to leaders. These are:

1. CliftonStrengths (formerly StrengthsFinder)
2. Myers–Briggs Type Indicator (MBTI)
3. DISC Assessment
4. Motivators Assessment (formerly PIAV Values Index)

CliftonStrengths

It's a fact of human nature that we tend to be unclear about our strengths; we aren't often encouraged to look at them. Instead, we focus on our flaws, or the things we feel we have to 'fix' about ourselves. When we're in deep dissonance, we focus on how to hide our flaws from other people and/or pretend they don't exist.

Deeply rooted in positive psychology, the CliftonStrengths assessment provides an antidote to that tendency. The online assessment consists of 177 paired statements; you choose which one best describes you. The assessment measures your talents – your natural patterns of thinking, feeling, and behaving. Your responses create your unique strengths profile based on 34 strength themes.

The CliftonStrengths research indicates that your most significant area for personal improvement isn't where you're weakest, but rather where you're strongest. Using this assessment, you can identify your greatest strengths – the things that make you stand out from the crowd – and focus on bringing them to the forefront in your everyday work and interactions.

I implemented CliftonStrengths at Atrion with incredible results. We started by putting 35 of our top-level leaders through the programme. This created a new awareness we could bring to our teams, and gave us a common language that we could use to get past the heightened emotions that often flare in challenging moments.

Next, we brought this assessment to our sales team. Soon, we started seeing an impressive uptick in revenue. By the time we sold the company, our sales team of ten people (three with less than two years' experience) were producing $168 million in annual sales. (For comparison's sake, the company that eventually acquired us had 140 salespeople generating about $340 million in sales.) Our NPS (Net Promoter Score) was 80, compared to an industry average of about 33. We were operating in the ranks of Disney and the Ritz Carlton – in large part due to the fact that our teams knew their strengths and how to use them.

Myers–Briggs Type Indicator (MBTI)

Derived from the personality studies conducted by C.G. Jung, the Myers–Briggs Type Indicator (MBTI) assessment categorizes people into one of 16 unique personality types based on four core indicators: introverted/extroverted, sensing/intuiting, thinking/feeling, and judging/perceiving. Which extreme you fall under in each of these four categories determines your overall personality type.

While somewhat general in scope, I find Myers–Briggs assessments very useful, because they target what fuels us and what we need in order to maintain internal balance.

For example, I was always told I was an extrovert because I like being around people. I can be somewhat gregarious, and I love speaking to groups. But for years, I avoided networking like the plague. Being in crowds exhausted me, but I couldn't figure out why. I used this as an excuse to avoid going to meetings and events, even when I knew doing so would move my company forwards.

Then, I took an MBTI assessment. Turns out, I'm an introvert – an INFP (introverted, intuitive, feeling, and prospecting), to be exact. I learned that, as an introvert and intuitive, I needed 'downtime' to recharge. It wasn't that I didn't like people; it was just that crowds weren't a source of energy for me. Knowing this helped me bust through my excuses and start networking more deliberately. I didn't need to avoid these events, I just needed to give myself a buffer on either side to get my energy and focus back. The result of this switch in perspective was that I made many incredible connections and Atrion became one of the most recognized brands in Rhode Island.

DISC Assessment

This assessment reveals who you are when you're at your most natural and unguarded, and who you are when you need to be 'on' for others.

DISC measures four dimensions of your behaviour: Decisive (problem-solving), Interactive (interaction and emotion), Stability (persistence and steadiness), and Cautious (procedures and protocols). Each quadrant is measured by a numeric score. You'll learn where you habitually shine, and where you habitually resist or rock the boat. Part of the assessment includes what roles are naturally suited to your personality, and which will challenge you.

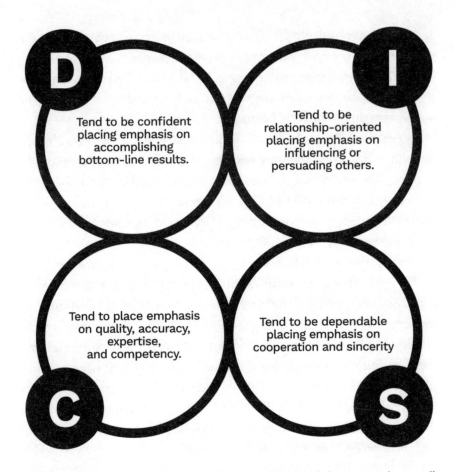

After taking my first DISC assessment, I learned that in my 'normal' mode – when I'm relaxed – I'm pure 'I'. I communicate in big-picture terms, my ideas are abstract and forward-looking, and I naturally fall into storytelling and exaggeration. When I'm in my 'operational' mode – when I'm at work, or when I'm stressed – I'm a high 'D'. It's all about action.

After learning this, I finally understood why I often had to repeat myself over and over to make my ideas understood, and why I was constantly looking for new ways to give directions to my staff. As a high 'I' I communicated in a way that was foreign to 75 per cent of my employees! When I was in 'D' mode, I was still reaching only a small percentage of the people who were trying to take direction from me.

What I took from the DISC Assessment was that I needed to craft my messages in a way that was accessible to all four communication styles. If I was only speaking at my natural high 'I' everyone else was at a disadvantage. I had to be less abstract, more detailed. I needed to include concrete, action-language for Ds, warmth and empathy for Ss, and lots of details for Cs. Once I implemented this, I noticed an immediate difference in how people responded to my communication.

Motivators Assessment (formerly PIAV Values Index)

This assessment often goes together with the DISC assessment. It's an analysis of what matters to you and what drives you to achieve the objectives you set for yourself.

Understanding your internal drivers and those of the people around you is key to fuelling growth. Some people are motivated by money and status, others by altruism, others by their desire to stand out as unique. Knowing what will push you to succeed helps you align your inner narrative to your goals.

When offered opportunities or positions that don't align with our motivators, we won't do our best work. For example, traditions aren't one of my primary motivators. Instead, I'm driven by learning, creating, and responding to ambitious challenges. Knowing my motivators helps me say no to people and opportunities that don't align with my vision.

After Atrion was sold, I had an opportunity to sit down with many of my former employees. When asked about their experience, most said something like, 'Even though we talked a lot about revenue and profits, we worked off a different balance sheet. We measured the impact on our employees, our clients, and the community. We could have made more money, but our legacy was more important.' This demonstrated our shared values as a company, and how attracting people with similar motivators can produce amazing results.

Other self-assessment tools

In the end, any tool or modality that provides you with insight into who you are and why you do the things you do is worth using. Some people like the concrete assessments I've mentioned above; others find value in more esoteric tools like the Enneagram, astrology, or Human Design.

Regardless of what tools call to you, I offer this piece of advice: knowing your tendencies is helpful; accepting them as absolute truth is not. There are kernels of wisdom in all assessments that will serve you, but there are also infinite variations within each type, strength, or category.

Why does this distinction matter? Because we never want to use information from our assessments as fodder for self-justification in moments of cognitive dissonance.

I've seen many people justify less-than-ideal personal and leadership choices based on things they 'knew' about themselves. For example, I've witnessed leaders who don't score high on 'soft skills' rationalize their callous treatment of employees because 'I'm just not one of those "connector" types.' (George from Chapter 2 is a perfect example of this.) I've seen others turn down career-exploding opportunities because they couldn't get past their introversion to speak on a stage.

You absolutely can do things you're not 'wired' for. You just need to do them creatively so that you don't cause more internal dissonance. Some of the most powerful public speakers I know are introverts. Some of the most self-reflective people I know are extroverts. Just because something doesn't come 'naturally' to you doesn't mean you should avoid it. In fact, learning those skills will almost always provide you with more opportunities for self-observation, learning, and growth.

Also keep in mind that within each assessment category or type lies a range of personalities, tendencies, and expressions. The way I do introversion isn't necessarily the way you will. The way you express your values won't necessarily line up with how others express them. For this reason, it's essential not to take anything you learn through assessments at face value. Instead, consider your results to be a map of the general area in which you're living; it shows you where you are, but has no bearing on where you can travel. Create Unguarded Moments to sift through and assimilate the useful information and work with any cognitive dissonance that arises.

In short, what helps to connect you to your superpowers is helpful. What gives you an excuse to get in your own way is not.

Step 4: assess your goals

Once we have created space for Unguarded Moments, got to know our inner world, and gathered objective information about our personalities, values, and strengths, we can start to look at our goals – personal, professional, and organizational.

Goals are funny: they seem objective, but in the end, they're deeply personal. Sometimes, when we come out of Ghost Mode and into a state of self-observation, we realize that we don't always want the things we said we wanted. Or, we see that we *do* want those things, but not for the reasons we imagined.

We will talk a lot more about goals and how to set them in Part III of this book, but for now, simply observe your goals through your lens of increasing self-awareness. Are they aligned with who you are and what you want, or are they 'shoulds'? Do they feel attainable, or are they more like wishes? If your goals are no longer aligned, set them aside. It's not helpful to waste time accomplishing tasks that aren't moving you forwards.

Step 5: get feedback

The best way for us to put our new self-awareness into perspective (and, ultimately, into action) is through feedback.

Feedback is one of the best ways to check in with your progress and target zones of cognitive dissonance. There's a science to asking for and receiving useful, productive feedback from the people in your life; we'll be taking a deep dive into that process in Chapter 8.

For now, though, I want to focus on a different form of feedback: the feedback of your environment. When we change, everything else changes too. When we stop reacting in certain ways, people change the way they react to us. Our new choices produce different outcomes. The result of looking inwards is an improved reality looking outwards.

As you go through the five steps to grow your self-awareness, notice how your actions create consequences. Notice that when you deliberately change or update something in your behaviour, it creates a cascade of shifts. My company's visibility skyrocketed when I became aware that I was using my inner dissonance around introversion to avoid networking, and instead found a way to do it that felt good. You, too, can use the new input you're receiving from self-awareness to make different choices and create different results.

The other great thing about getting feedback is that it shows you that perception is everything. The experience you have might be markedly different than that of your employee, customer, or client.

Early in my career, I was doing a 'cut-over' for Polaroid Corporation – a reworking of their internal telephone system. At any point in time, this client had about 6,000 phone calls flowing through their system, so taking it down for even a little while was a major challenge. We scheduled the cut-over for 2.00 a.m.; I would have exactly two hours to take down the system, pull the old stuff out, install the new system, get it running, and get all the calls routed again.

Of course, we ran into a problem – a pretty intense one, too. I found myself working side by side with our contact, whose name was Dave, to troubleshoot the issue. The thing was, Dave wanted to go left, and I wanted to go right – and I *knew* his way would fail to solve the problem and blow our deadline.

So, I took over. I won't say that I pushed the guy aside, but I did kind of ignore him. Maybe I was even a little … abrupt. But at this point, we had only minutes left to make the deadline. It was my way or the highway.

To cut a long story short, we got the new system up and working by the deadline. I heaved a sigh of relief and patted myself on the back. Mission accomplished.

The next day, I talked to my business partner on the phone.

'How did last night go?' he asked.

'Great! We ran into a few snags, but we got it done, and everything works.'

'Well, I just followed up with our contact. They agree that everything works, and they're happy with the solution. But Dave thinks you're a jackass.'

'What?' I was shocked. I might have been a little short with Dave at the end, but we got the job done. What was his problem?

I wanted to snap that Dave was totally off-base, that I'd been justified in overriding him – that I was right, and *he* was the jackass. But instead, I took a deep breath and asked my partner, 'What was his perspective?'

The fact was, there were probably three or four people in the whole US who could have solved the issue with that cut-over and still met the deadline – and two of them were my business partner and me. But when I thought about it, the fact that we solved the problem wasn't the issue. It was the way I handled Dave. I treated him as though he was in my way, when I could have – and should have – taken two extra minutes to include him in the process.

That event changed my entire approach to dealing with clients. From then on, I chose to engage with clients during difficult situations instead of pushing them away – even when doing so cost me time.

Receiving feedback is tough. Often, we're tempted to dismiss others' perspectives and get on with our lives. But if we want to become more self-aware (and apply that awareness to leadership), we need to realize that we don't operate in a bubble. We are constantly engaging with other people in a complicated series of interactions and relationships – and we can't discount those others if we want to be successful as leaders.

Again, we'll tackle this in depth in Chapter 8, but for now, notice how you react when feedback is presented. Do you clam up? Lash out? Go into dissonance? Start making the other person wrong? Or can you listen and receive it objectively?

Putting awareness to work

A great place to begin to apply the fruits of your self-observation is in moments when you need to make a choice. It can be a big choice, or a small one that occurs in the normal stream of your day. When a moment arises, ask yourself, 'What am I choosing right now, and why?'

As leaders, we're faced with these moments of choice all the time. When we recognize them, we can be more intentional about them. We can see where cognitive dissonance is occurring and interrupt the cycle of self-justification. We can ask ourselves, 'Is there something I need to do differently to create the result I want?'

I once mentored a young woman named Amy who had just been promoted to team lead at a customer service company. She'd been with her company for less than a year, and suddenly found herself in a direct supervisory position leading people who'd been there for decades. Most of her team respected and liked her, but there was one woman who did not.

The woman had been with the organization for more than 15 years, and made it quite clear that Amy had nothing to teach her about how to do her job. She talked over Amy in meetings, became belligerent when Amy gave her feedback, and let the entire office know that she wasn't going to take orders from someone half her age.

As you can imagine, this was a highly uncomfortable situation for Amy, who was doing her best to support her team and fill her predecessor's shoes.

When we spoke about it, I asked her, 'Why do you think they promoted you?'

'Honestly, I'm not sure. I'm good with the customers, I guess.'

'Why do you feel so intimidated by this person on your team?'

'I don't know that either,' she replied. 'I just do. She's aggressive, and mean, and tries to make me look stupid. I don't understand why she hates me so much!'

'You deal with aggressive clients on the phone all day long, and you don't bat an eye. What's different about this woman?'

Amy could only shake her head.

I invited her to sit with the question over the weekend. 'Ask yourself, "Why am I intimidated?" And then, every time you think you have an answer, ask it again. Go a layer deeper.'

This process of asking the same question over and over again is called 'recursive questioning'. It invites us to exhaust our surface-level responses, justifications, and excuses, and expose what's really going on. Amy did the recursive questioning process I recommended, and by the end of the weekend she'd come to some key realizations.

'I'm intimidated by her because I don't feel like I deserve this promotion,' she told me. 'Every time this woman challenges me, part of me feels like she's right. I can't handle this. I'm not qualified to be in charge.'

'What else?'

'I don't like conflict. So I haven't been holding her accountable or calling her out. And I feel like I'm taking everything personally, even when I know I shouldn't.'

Honestly, I was shocked that she'd come so far with her awareness in just a few days. 'What are you going to do with this information?' I asked.

'It's not about whether she likes me or not,' Amy replied. 'I'm the team lead, and I need to own it.'

Over the next several months, Amy settled into her role admirably. Her team was getting stellar results, and her confidence grew. Her employee's animosity didn't go away, but she stopped taking it personally. Instead, she started asking for constructive feedback from other team members, and used the results to improve her leadership skills.

When the woman finally crossed a line with a client that Amy couldn't ignore, Amy was ready to act. She called her employee into her office and asked her to sit down. 'Here's what I'm observing,' she said, and proceeded to lay out the facts in a deliberate, calm manner. 'Now, here's what I need from you. I need you to address these issues around how you connect with clients. I need you to be more respectful in team meetings. I need you to be more supportive of our team, because we're all in this together. And I need you to be more accountable, so I'm putting you on a 60-day plan.'

Not surprisingly, the woman didn't take this feedback well. Within 60 days, Amy was forced to terminate her – but she did so with compassion, clarity, and the clear knowledge that it was the right move not just for her personally, but for her whole team. The intimidation she once felt was no longer a factor in her decision-making process.

It was amazing to witness how one piece of awareness led to so much change.

A year later, I asked Amy the same question that had sparked her entire growth process. 'Why do you think you got that promotion?'

This time, she concisely and unselfconsciously listed all the strengths that made her shine in her role. She was fabulous with clients. She was a quick and effective problem-solver. She was a great team player. And she knew how to navigate conflict without compromising her integrity.

It would have been easy for Amy to look outwards and blame her employee for being a jerk. It would have been an easy position to justify. But that wouldn't have helped her grow into her new role as a team leader. In fact, it would have kept her spinning her wheels in that space of 'I don't deserve this job' – a space dissonant to what she really wanted, which was to be an effective leader.

Instead, she looked inwards, and it changed everything. She made space for self-observation through Unguarded Moments. She collected information about herself. She evaluated that information and compared it to her goals. She resolved the dissonance between what she was feeling and thinking and what she wanted to achieve. Moreover, she integrated the feedback she received as she put the changes into play.

Deliberate self-questioning is one of our best tools for accessing the deep currents of our inner world. It can show us where we feel dissonance, where we are justifying, and where we need to shift our perspective.

In the last section of this chapter, I've created a list of questions you can work with as you begin this process. Some are targeted towards uncovering dissonance; others are intended to help you see your strengths more clearly. Choose the ones that feel like they're pushing your buttons, or create new ones to support what you're observing in your Unguarded Moments.

Once you have some golden nuggets in hand from your questioning sessions, hold them up to the light. Do these thoughts, patterns, habits, or beliefs support your goals? Do they move you forwards? Are they even true?

Amy's self-questioning led her not only to the core of the feelings her employee was triggering inside her, but also to the realization that her 'worthiness' to lead was nothing more than a matter of perspective. *It was up to her to decide* whether she was capable. What mattered wasn't what her employee thought of her, but what she thought of herself. Once she changed her perspective, she became more confident, which in turn transformed her decision-making process. In the end, this benefitted her whole team.

The real reason awareness matters

'OK,' you may be thinking, 'I'm on board with this. The more I know myself, the more intentional I can get with my choices. Makes sense. But what's the big picture? Why do my intentional choices matter to anyone but me?'

Well, my friend, they matter because companies are driven by leaders. And when leaders don't look inwards it's not only their teams that suffer. Their customers, their shareholders, and their bottom lines are also impacted.

Remember when Apple first released the iPhone? While Steve Jobs was celebrating his achievement at MacWorld 2007, Steve Ballmer, the head honcho at Microsoft, was being interviewed at a press conference. 'Five hundred dollars?' Ballmer laughed. 'That's the most expensive phone in the world! And it doesn't appeal to business customers because it doesn't have a keyboard, which makes it not a very good email machine.'

Well, millions of people bought that $500 phone. And Microsoft never came close to catching up in the smartphone market.

The media panned Ballmer for that interview for nearly a decade. Looking back, it was a moment where self-awareness would have served far better than the time-honoured business strategy of badmouthing your competition. Ultimately, it was rumoured that Ballmer's slow response to the new era of mobile technology drove him out of Microsoft.

It's my opinion that self-awareness on the part of leadership could have gone a long way towards salvaging Microsoft's market share. But decision makers spent too much time trying to justify their position (aka, their cognitive dissonance), and not enough time examining their motivations for that position. Had they looked inwards, they might have seen what Apple saw – an opportunity to serve their customers in a whole new way.

Here's another example. Back in the day, Blockbuster Video stores were everywhere. There were more than 4,500 stores in the US alone. Despite their convenient locations, they made nearly 16 per cent of their revenue from late fees – because while renting videos was a high priority for busy people, returning them was not. Then, along came a little company called Netflix. You could order your video online, get it shipped to your door and return it whenever the heck you felt like it. No late fees. No extra trips. You just couldn't order a new movie until you'd sent back the old one.

This new company disrupted Blockbuster's entire model. As the online side of things developed, Netflix adapted to offer streaming services. In 2000, they approached Blockbuster with an offer to sell

Netflix for about $50 million. Genius, right? That partnership would have combined the strengths of both companies and made Blockbuster viable for decades to come. But Blockbuster's leadership looked at that proposal and said, 'No way.' Instead, they inked a 20-year deal to deliver on-demand movies with Enron Broadband Services, a subsidiary of energy trading giant Enron.

Because Blockbuster was so externally focused, they didn't see that their business model was going the way of the dinosaurs. They didn't have the right model to create a streaming service. They would have been better off acquiring someone who already knew how to do it – but in Netflix, they didn't see an asset and ally. They only saw a small-time usurper coming in to snatch their market share.

Well, you know how the rest of the story goes. Within five years, Blockbuster was closing stores around the country. Their streaming service was so poorly designed that they lost half of their original customers within the first 90 days. Netflix, on the other hand, was becoming a household name – the go-to streaming service for movies and TV. 'Bingeing' shows on Netflix became the new thing to do on a Friday night.

Businesses are unique entities, but the way that businesses see themselves in the world comes directly from their leadership. If leadership isn't inward-looking, self-aware and open to change, they won't be able to identify what's not working. They won't know which choices will move them intentionally towards their long-term goals, and which will make them go Blockbuster.

History proves that nearly every time a company chooses an outward-looking, fixed mindset over an inward-looking, growth-oriented mindset, that company loses. At the end of the day, we fail as leaders when we hold ourselves back from adaptability and innovation – and the only way to know what needs to be adapted, changed, or scrapped entirely is to remove the distortion of Ghost Mode and cognitive dissonance.

If we can't see ourselves clearly, we can't see our organizations clearly. We can't lean forwards into the big, meaningful challenges. We can't identify the right kinds of risks. And we can't lead with intention.

When we're externally focused, we look to the world to create the opportunity for us to have Decisive and Defining Moments that move us forwards. We can find ourselves waiting for everything to line up just so – for life to give us the chance to make the right decisions. But I think, deep down, you know how rarely that happens.

When we balance our external orientation with inward focus, we realize that we can't understand our decision-making process until we understand ourselves. To make the right decisions – to lead with intention and integrity – we have to become clear about our motivations and resolve the dissonances that prompt us into knee-jerk reactions instead of creative solutions.

So, ponder this: what decisions will you make in the next 30 days? And what do you want to understand about yourself before you make them?

* * *

There's a popular proverb that says: 'The best time to plant a tree was 20 years ago. The second-best time is now.' That applies to self-knowledge as well. It's never too late to get to know who you are and what you stand for. It's never too late to resolve your inner dissonances, and start being authentic in your leadership and life.

Reflection

- Life comes at us hard and fast. It's imperative that we, as leaders, choose how we will respond. There is no leadership 'playbook'; all we have is our awareness and our ability to understand the moment. It's not our job to decide how we learn. It's our job to *decide to learn when the opportunity presents itself.*

- Presence invites and perpetuates *self-awareness*, which is the first and most crucial step to emerging from Ghost Mode into Intentional Leadership.
- *The five steps to grow your self-awareness*: create space through Unguarded Moments; connect to your inner world; collect objective information; assess your goals; ask for feedback.
- Companies are driven by leaders. When leaders don't look inwards, it's not only their teams that suffer. Their customers, their shareholders, and their bottom lines are also impacted.
- We can't navigate effectively in our outer world if we are blind to what shapes our inner world.
- Cognitive dissonance is a gift. It draws our attention to an area where growth is needed.
- History proves that nearly every time a company chooses an outward-looking, fixed mindset over an inward-looking, growth-oriented mindset, that company loses.
- Apply the fruits of your self-observation in moments when you need to make a choice. It can be a big choice, or a small one that occurs in the normal stream of your day. When a moment arises, ask yourself, 'What am I choosing right now, and why?'
- The best way to get to know yourself is simply to *be* with yourself, without any distractions.

Unity of Thought and Action

Thought – begin to cultivate awareness

We navigate myriad challenges and opportunities in our lives. Sometimes we are self-aware enough to be fully present, but other times we simply go through the motions. When we're on autopilot and not showing up, we become our own worst enemies. We struggle with the resulting cognitive dissonance by justifying our actions, judging others by how they respond, and building a narrative that supports our point of view. Where has cognitive dissonance shown up for you in your leadership journey? How can you apply the knowledge from this chapter to change your perspective?

Action – create Unguarded Moments

The following are simple practices you can work with to integrate the five steps to grow your self-awareness into your daily life and routine.

You can work with these questions using the recursive questioning method described earlier in this chapter, or sit with a single question in your daily meditation. Each question will lead you to a new level of self-awareness, which you can then integrate with the objective information you've gathered, your goals assessment and the feedback you receive from others and your environment. Choose one question a day to work with for a period of two weeks. If the questions below don't resonate, write your own list.

1. What do I like about myself the most?
2. What do I value the most in life?
3. What am I trying to achieve, and am I achieving those goals?
4. What am I doing that is working or going well?
5. What am I doing that is slowing me down?
6. What has changed about me in the last ten years?
7. What am I taking for granted?
8. Do I feel in control of myself, and what do I do when I'm not?
9. Am I living in a way that feels true to myself?
10. What am I holding on to that I need to let go of?
11. What have I given up on?
12. When did I last push the boundaries of my comfort zone?
13. What's the one thing I'd like others to remember about me at the end of my life?
14. Am I being called to change – and if yes, how so?

CHAPTER 4

Core Ideology: The Foundation of Trust

'Do not go where the path may lead; instead, go where there is no path and leave a trail.' – Emerson

When I was in my early twenties, I worked for a Rhode Island-based technology company as the senior director of Technical Services. When I started there as a lowly test engineer, it was a family-owned company with a strong culture that I felt great about supporting. However, over time, the culture shifted to become more focused on the bottom line than on people and values.

Since I was in a management position and making decisions on a day-to-day basis, I found myself having to say and do things that were totally out of alignment with the kind of person I was and wanted to be. It wasn't a comfortable place to be.

Two things happened in quick succession that pushed me over the edge. The first was on the Friday before Thanksgiving. I was called to the reception area over the overhead paging system. As I approached the front desk, I was greeted by an older gentleman named Ned, the owner/operator of a local landscaping business. During our very awkward conversation, he informed me that he was here to repossess the Christmas decorations that my company had ordered from him over a month ago.

What the heck? My confusion must have been apparent because Ned launched into the whole sordid story at top volume. Evidently, our Christmas décor had come with a whopping $7,000 price tag, and the CEO of our company had stiffed Ned on the bill. Being that seven grand was most of a month's income for Ned, he wasn't about to let my boss get away with this.

Just a few days before, my CEO had given us a pep talk using phrases like, 'This is going to be the best Christmas ever!' Now, it was looking like the *worst* Christmas ever … for my team and me, but especially for Ned, who was still fuming on the other side of the reception desk.

Of course, I had to let Ned in. As we went from room to room, tearing down garlands and relieving the windowsills of poinsettias, part of me was writhing in shame that our company would treat another local business owner this way. Another part of me was cheering Ned on. Coming here to repossess a bunch of plants took serious guts.

The second wake-up call happened the following Monday. I had travelled to Washington, D.C. for a critical client meeting. I was scheduled to come back early the next day, but around noon I got a call from my boss saying, 'I need you back here as soon as possible.' I did the meeting, caught the next available flight to Providence, and arrived at our headquarters just before 9.00p.m. When I walked in the door, my boss grabbed my arm and hissed in my ear.

'The bank is going to foreclose on this building. They're coming here to put a padlock on the door within days. We found a new space in Massachusetts, but we need to move everything out of here before they shut us down, and no one can know about it. I hope you had some coffee on the flight, cause we're going to be here a while.'

Suddenly, the whole situation with Ned made a bit more sense. I asked myself, 'What kind of person orders seven grand's worth of Christmas decorations when he's about to be foreclosed on?' Was this an organization and leader I wanted to work for and to be associated with?

The answer, of course, was no. Driving home in the early-morning hours, I knew this was beyond what I could live with – but I felt trapped. I had a young family, and we were new homeowners. Christmas was coming – and everyone knows that the holiday season is the worst time to look for a new job. How could I just leave?

I felt like I was in a crucible, forced to choose between virtue and survival. But when I boiled it down, the choice was pretty simple: leave my job and face the potentially dire consequences, or stay and lose all respect for myself. The next day, I tendered my resignation.

On Thanksgiving morning, the reality of what I had done set in. We had an unembellished Thanksgiving. Facing the terrifying repercussions of my choice, we were determined to save every cent. We had a modest financial cushion, but nowhere enough to see us through an extensive job search.

The following week, I connected with my good friend Charlie, who had started a small IT business called Atrion and was struggling to get his operation running smoothly. I was toying with the idea of starting my own company but wasn't sure if I had enough capital to get it off the ground – or enough time to source that funding before my savings ran out. During our conversation, we joked about what two highly capable individuals could accomplish if they joined forces.

The rest, as they say, is history. Our two-person operation became a multiple-award-winning company with 268 dedicated employees and annual revenues of more than $168 million.

Looking back, I can see that my drive home from that clandestine moving session was an Unguarded Moment. I looked inside myself to determine what I wanted, and made a choice based on that knowledge.

The choice to leave my job was a huge turning point – a Decisive Moment. And joining my friend in creating Atrion was a Defining Moment. If I'd made the 'safe' choice and looked for another job in my field as an employee, I would have had a very different life and career.

At the time, things weren't so clear. When I decided to resign, I wasn't choosing the path to my final position as the CEO of a multi-million-dollar company. I wasn't choosing a bright, shiny future over a soul-sucking job. At that time, I had *no idea* what the future held; bar a few lucky connections and lots of hard work, I could have ended up jobless, lost my new house, negatively impacted my family, and left my big American dream in shambles.

No, when I resigned with everything on the line, I wasn't choosing an outcome, or even a possibility. I was choosing *who I knew myself to be* over who I would have become if I'd stayed. In other words, I was choosing my *Core Ideology* and obeying my *inner authority*.

Your Core Ideology: the iron string

Although they may have different ways of expressing the concept, it's my opinion that all great leaders operate from a place of clear, well-defined Core Ideology. They follow their instincts and stay true to their values, even when everyone around them is going the opposite way. Even if they never talk about 'values' or 'purpose', we know what they stand for because their words and actions make it clear.

Deep down, I think we all want to have that kind of conviction. And yet, most of the people I encounter in my leadership programmes have *no idea* what their Core Ideology is. They're not even aware that they need one.

The concept of ideology was first introduced during the French Revolution to mean 'the science of ideas'. In his 1971 essay, 'On the Concept of Ideology in Political Science', Willard A. Mullins suggests that ideology is composed of the following four essential characteristics:

1. It must have power over cognition.
2. It must be capable of guiding one's evaluations.
3. It must provide guidance towards actions.
4. It must be logically coherent.

In business circles, 'core ideology' is a term for the belief system that defines an organization's identity. However, I believe Core Ideology is something we embody in every moment as leaders. It's a definitive statement of what you stand for, why you do what you do, and where you are going. In other words, it defines your leadership journey.

As an Intentional Leader, your Core Ideology will be highly meaningful to you. It will guide you, inspire you, and be unique to you as an individual. More, it will always reflect these three foundational truths:

1. Your *core values,* which are the *foundation* of your ideology.
2. Your *purpose,* which is the *expression* of your ideology.
3. Your *vision,* which is the *manifestation* of your ideology.

When you create clarity around these three components, you will have connected to your inner code of law – your *inner authority.* Your Core Ideology is the deep current of your life and leadership – the barometer by which you will measure all of your choices, the iron string that vibrates with self-trust. It's the deep place you can go to to regain your balance when the daily waves and storms of leadership threaten to push you off-course.

When our choices and actions are congruent with our Core Ideology, our decision-making processes are streamlined. We stop tolerating things that don't reflect our ideology (such as landscaper-stiffing CEOs and midnight office relocations, for example). When challenges come up, we can respond deliberately, from the stable foundation of our core values, purpose, and vision, rather than merely reacting in the moment. The more we lean into our Core Ideology, the more we will get to know ourselves, and the more nuanced our ideology will become. It's an ever-deepening, self-refining feedback loop.

And when Intentional Leadership calls us to deviate from the status quo, we will trust ourselves to go where there is no path, and blaze a trail.

On the other hand, before we become self-aware, our (undefined) ideology is often in conflict with our daily thoughts, feelings, and behaviours. We might realize that what we value most is in direct conflict with our habitual words and actions. This strands us in Ghost Mode, in a place of reactionary behaviour and lack of trust for ourselves and others. This absence of trust and direction impacts our experience as leaders as well as the experiences of our teams and organizations at large.

You see, a strong Core Ideology is the foundation of trust – and trust is the currency of leadership. I think of trust as a lifeline – a rope that everyone in an organization can hold on to. Many leaders try to lead from behind, pushing people towards a goal or vision that feels murky and undefined. 'Just keep going and you'll see,' they say. But, as you may have gleaned from this visual, it's pretty much impossible to push a rope forwards in a straight line.

As leaders, we need to be out in front. We need to have a secure connection to our Core Ideology so we know where we're going. We need to pull that line and keep everyone moving towards a shared vision.

If I don't know and trust myself as a leader, I'm not pulling that rope. I'm not in the driver's seat. I'm not moving things forwards. And, as others become aware that I don't have a clear destination, their desire to follow me is impacted.

In this chapter, I'll break down the three components of Core Ideology – values, purpose, and vision – and explore how each one functions within us as individuals as well as at an organizational level. Then, I'll share how we can begin to use our self-awareness and Core Ideology to break out of the reactionary space of Ghost Mode and lead in a more deliberate, intentional way.

Core Ideology builds inner authority

We learned in Chapter 3 that awareness is the antidote to the first symptom of Ghost Mode: lack of presence. What happens when we become more self-aware? We start to understand what makes us tick. We get clarity on what makes us unique, and what our strengths are. We get glimpses of the 'why' of ourselves.

As we get to know ourselves more deeply, we may begin to feel a rising sense of imbalance or disconnection. We're learning what matters to us, but we don't yet understand how to engage with it in a meaningful way. We're still in the surface-level space, facing each struggle as though it's a new wave and not part of a vast ocean. We repeat the same mistakes, habits, and rituals that we always have – only now, we carry a vague sense of unease that our actions are moving us further away from what we want rather than towards it. We wonder if we're steering the boat, or if we're just caught in a rip tide. We may even start to lose trust in ourselves, because we're now aware of where we're not honouring our internal commitment to what we believe matters.

If this is familiar to you, too, don't worry. It's a natural part of the learning curve. In fact, it's your sign that it's time to address the second symptom of Ghost Mode – reactionism and lack of trust – by identifying your Core Ideology and strengthening your inner authority.

There's a difference between reaction and response. One is habitual, instinctive, and serves the needs of the moment. The other is deliberate, considered, and aligned with a bigger vision. One strands you in Ghost Mode, fighting the waves; the other moves you into the deeper currents of Intentional Leadership.

When we identify and define what we stand for, and allow that truth to guide our decision-making and actions, we establish inner authority – a deep, well-founded trust in ourselves. We also dispel cognitive dissonance by creating congruence between what we think, what we say, and what we do. When challenges come up, we can respond deliberately, from the stable foundation of our core values, purpose, and vision, rather than merely reacting.

The more we practise this, the more reliable our inner authority will become. We will trust ourselves to make better, more aligned choices in even the most chaotic situations. We will see that our words and actions are congruent with our thoughts, values, and beliefs. And when Intentional Leadership calls us to deviate from the status quo, we will trust ourselves to go where there is no path and blaze a trail.

Values: the foundation of your Core Ideology

The term 'values' gets thrown around a lot in the business world. But despite its ubiquity, the concept of values is not well understood or leveraged correctly in most organizations.

There are many kinds of values (as I'll share later in this section), but the set of values we'll be focusing on are your core values. Core values are the bedrock of your Core Ideology; without them, you can't create (or sustain) your purpose and vision, which form the 'actionable' parts of your ideology.

I define core values as *the fundamental beliefs of a person, group, or organization.* These ideals are our guideposts for understanding the difference between right and wrong. They are the non-negotiable principles at the centre of every action and decision, and while they might evolve with time, they don't change with circumstances. And, most of all, we must be willing to make sacrifices to uphold them. If you had an inner compass, your values would be your True North.

Chances are, you already know at least one or two of your core values just from reading that description. You might value honesty, creativity, or community. You might value learning, tradition, or financial stability.

On the surface, the idea of core values seems simple. But in a Decisive Moment, knowing your core values can mean the difference between leading intentionally and reacting without foresight. For example, in a meeting, you may need to choose between letting the newest member of your team be heard or shutting her down because you're anxious to move on to the next action item. If you value innovation, letting her speak is the best choice (even if you're impatient), because you're committed to being open to new ideas no matter where they come from. If your value is efficiency, you might choose to say, 'Hold that thought, but be sure to write it down so we can discuss it later.'

The important thing is that, when you are in touch with your core values, you know what choices you're making and why. Your decisions will be more consistent. And you'll no longer miss Decisive Moments because you're stuck on autopilot.

Are you making values-based leadership decisions?

As we discussed earlier in this chapter, our core values can and should be a significant factor in all of our decisions as leaders. But for most of us, core values aren't at the forefront when we're under pressure.

I do an exercise with my workshop attendees that puts the importance of our values into perspective. I ask everyone to get a fresh sheet of paper. Then, I say, 'I'm going to give you 10 seconds to write down your top five values. Ready, set…Go!'

When the buzzer goes off, some people start writing furiously. Others freeze like deer in headlights. Others scowl at their papers. And while everyone struggles to connect with what I've asked them to do, I count down the remaining seconds, loudly.

'Five. Four. Three…'

By the time I yell 'One!' pretty much everyone is either laughing out loud or pissed off at me.

'That wasn't fair,' they'll say. 'You didn't give us any time to think about it! Who writes that fast?'

'I know,' I respond. 'It *wasn't* fair. But let me ask you: as a leader, how many decisions do you make in under 10 seconds every day? If you don't know your core values well enough to write them down while you're distracted, what are you basing all those decisions on? What's your anchor? What's your ideology?'

The fact is, we all make hundreds, even thousands, of decisions every day. And if we're making them without connection to or consideration for our core values, we are flailing in the ocean without oars or an anchor – and so are our teams, peers, and clients. They are at the mercy of our confusion and inconsistency.

Your core values are your true north

To me, the two most important things we can know about ourselves as leaders are:

1. What we value.
2. What we are willing to do to stay true to those values.

For core values to be core values, we must be willing to make sacrifices to stay true to them (like leaving a job where you're being asked to lead in an unethical manner). Otherwise, they're just ideas. Aspirations. Wannabes.

This is where many leaders and organizations get mixed up. There are core values – the building blocks of your Core Ideology that we're discussing in this section – and then there are other kinds of values.

In his book *The Advantage: Why Organizational Health Trumps Everything Else in Business,* Peter Lencioni describes these other values in several ways.

- *Aspirational values* are values or attributes that we would like to have, but which aren't natural, authentic, or even available to us. They must be 'managed' into existence.
- *Permission-to-play values* are those we adopt when we want to be accepted into a group. They're the things we say because it will help

us close a deal or get closer to a prospect. They're the lowest common denominator of our inner value system.

- *Accidental or unintentional values* arise over time without being developed by us or our teams. They aren't the things we put on our websites, but they're the deep currents that exist in our organization and drive behaviours. Under good leadership, these values can be beneficial, but more often, they're negative, even toxic.

None of these secondary values connects us to our Core Ideology or the truth of who we are. And yet, when it comes to everyday decision-making, these lesser values often drive our choices.

When we aren't in touch with our core values, we make reactionary choices that solve the issues of the moment but ultimately don't feel right to us. We can't pinpoint *why* they feel wrong, so we justify them to ourselves, perpetuating our inner dissonance.

Without core values, we also lose the ability to perceive the depth of our problems. For example: is our unhappiness at work a surface-level issue that could be reframed to help us feel more purposeful, or is it a fundamental misalignment that can't be solved through compromise? Are we resisting our new company policies because they feel restrictive, or because we substantively disagree with them?

We often spin in circles when we could walk in a straight line towards our goals. The solution to this 'dizziness' is to engage your self-awareness and clarify your core values. Once you know what they are, regard them as indisputable and self-evident. Draw a line in your mind between your core values and everything else.

The wonderful thing is, when we treat our core values as our True North, even the most complex and scary decisions – such as leaving our jobs with no back-up plan, initiating difficult conversations, or taking a position we aren't fully qualified for – become cut-and-dry. They're either aligned or they're not.

So, if you're up against a difficult choice, ask yourself: 'What are my core values? Which choice would best help me express them? What am

I willing to give up to stay true to them? What am I willing to tolerate, and what is a deal-breaker for me?'

I promise, when you start practising this, you'll feel a surge of confidence and self-trust almost immediately.

The role of values within organizations

Do you know what your company's core values are? Sadly, most of the companies I work with don't have a clue. And just as a lack of knowledge about our personal values fosters reactionism, lack of direction, and cognitive dissonance in our daily decision-making, vague or undefined company values create those same issues at an organizational level.

Core values within a company determine everything: how clients are served, how services are created and delivered, how employees are hired and fired, and how internal disputes are resolved. If a company's leadership team has no decision-making process, it falls to individual leaders to do what seems best in the moment. The result is like a fleet of ships, each with its own captain, all of whom want to end up in the same place but insist on sailing in different directions to get there. It reminds me of Odysseus's journey home after the Trojan War. One bad decision after another sent Odysseus and his 12 ships on a 10-year journey of death, destruction, and trouble.

Organizations without defined core values operate in Ghost Mode. They may be adept at solving the problems of the moment, but lack momentum in the long term. They often have higher employee turnover rates, lower productivity, and are less innovative than companies with defined core values. Leaders at multiple levels are left to their own devices – or worse, expected to enforce conflicting policies and expectations. It's the polar opposite of Intentional Leadership.

Creating core values within your organization allows everyone in management to lead more intentionally. Clarity creates a concrete metric for decision-making, and a foundation for ethics in employee, contractor, partner, and customer relationships. When core values are defined, everything suddenly becomes more transparent. Systems are either explained or invalidated. Lines are drawn. Dissonance is minimized and trust is built.

After reading this, I'll bet you can think of at least five companies with clear, defined core values right off the bat. Examples such as Starbucks, Patagonia, State Farm Insurance, Zappos, and Apple come to mind. As a customer, you know what these companies stand for. Their values are part of everything, from their branding to their management style to their product creation and distribution. It's no coincidence that these companies have some of the highest rates of employee retention and satisfaction, as well as a dedicated customer base. People connect to organizations that value the same things they do.

In my career, I have worked for several companies that lacked clarity around their core values. My personal experience was that this created higher stress, anxiety, and burnout situations. I'll bet you can also think of (or have worked for) companies that don't have clear core values. These are companies that put their values on their website but not on the boardroom table. Their actions aren't consistent or transparent. Employees see the disconnection and hypocrisy. Stakeholders don't believe leadership means what they say. Trust deteriorates. Some people might make money, but in the end, no one wins.

A lack of core values also creates a breeding ground for the self-serving and cowardly behaviours that allows tyrants and unethical leaders to rise to power. How many people knew about Harvey Weinstein's behaviour and said nothing? How many at Enron knew what they were doing was illegal, but contributed anyway, because no one else was holding the line? Values give leaders a backbone. They make us accountable.

Purpose: the expression of your Core Ideology

Research has shown that when individuals develop and pursue their purpose, they are happier, more content, and experience greater general well-being. Their lives have meaning, and meaning creates momentum.

Organizations that are able to create purpose and meaning experience higher employee engagement, accelerated growth, and increased profitability.

There's a lot of talk in the leadership community about purpose and the 'Big Why'. While I love these discussions, I think we are overcomplicating them.

So many people I know – from entry-level workers to senior-level leaders – are dissatisfied with their work lives. They are challenged to find meaning in the work they do. They repeatedly say things like, 'Beyond working with our customers, pleasing our shareholders, and earning a pay cheque, I don't know why I'm working. What's the point of it all?'

Many of these people feel that they're not making a difference. They are having limited, if any, impact on those around them. They feel lost in the machine – and worse, their lack of fulfilment and meaning seeps into their personal lives and relationships as well. They're waiting for someone to come along and lift them up, but no one is coming.

I'm not a person who believes in predestination or fate. Core purpose is not something that we search for and find. We create and shape our own purpose, and it's something we cultivate and solidify over time. We choose it – and then, we embrace it, embody it, and lead with it in every aspect of our lives. And so, my answer to the profound, existential question of purpose is incredibly simple: *your purpose is to perpetuate the things you value.*

Put simply, if you value service, your purpose is to perpetuate service – through kindness, caring, and thoughtful action. If you value abundance, your purpose is to perpetuate wealth for yourself, and for everyone around you. If you value honesty, your work is to perpetuate truth and dismantle lies.

It's a bit like blowing up a balloon: at first, it consumes a lot of work and energy as you push past constriction. But eventually, as the energy (breath) you put into it increases, it expands. It takes up space in the world. And it has meaning to those who see and touch it. But walking the talk isn't easy. In fact, it's one of the hardest things we can do as leaders.

The great thing about choosing and building your purpose is that, once you know what you're creating, you can share it. As an Intentional Leader, your purpose generates passion within you and everyone around you – and passion is contagious. By creating meaning in your life, you allow your work to grow beyond you and create meaning in others' lives.

Using your core values as your barometer, you can bring purpose to everything you do, no matter your vocation. But first, you'll need to narrow down not only what your purpose is, but how you most want to express it.

Defining your purpose

As I shared above, purpose isn't something mystical or bestowed; it's something we create by perpetuating our values. But how can we turn our values into a purpose we can express in the world? And how do we distil our idea into something we can easily communicate to others?

When I work with clients on this topic, I like to start by getting a general sense of their interests, strengths, motivators, relationships, and leadership tendencies – in essence, I walk them through the work we did around self-awareness in Chapter 3. Next, we focus on core values to distil the person's chosen purpose.

Before we get into that process, let's take a more in-depth look at motivation. (If you took a Motivators Assessment based on our discussion in Chapter 3, those results might be helpful here!) Not everyone is catalyzed by the same things, and forcing your purpose through a channel that doesn't inspire you will send you into Ghost Mode in no time.

In their book *Conscious Capitalism*, John Mackey and Raj Sisodia introduced the idea that there are four main categories of 'purpose'. I have taken these themes and adapted them specifically to Intentional Leadership.

The Five Core Expressions of Purpose are:

1. Knowledge: higher education and learning; the ongoing acquisition of information; turning information into meaningful insights; facilitating the expansion of knowledge in the world.
2. Service: building relationships; improving others' lives through nurturing, caregiving, acknowledgement, appreciation and acts of service.
3. Accomplishment: building systems, processes, and organizations; accumulation of wealth and material items for self and others; professional attainment and social status; creating beauty in a tangible format (i.e. through art); building something concrete and lasting.
4. Impact: changemaking; seeking innovation, evolution, and disruptive change; executing a long-term vision for global improvement; dismantling outdated structures.
5. Belief: serving a cause; seeking spiritual knowledge or attunement; connection with a higher force, power, or ideal.

Those who fall into the 'Impact' category won't be motivated by things like money, beauty, or learning for learning's sake. They want to change the world, and the only things that 'stick' with them are the tools that help them do that (I know this, because this is my category). On the other hand, someone who falls into the 'Service' category won't find meaning by accumulating money or knowledge either, except where those things intersect with the reward they feel from helping others and seeing them grow.

The lesson here: if you're not motivated by the same things as the people around you, that doesn't mean you're not able to be purposeful. You can't mimic – or live – someone else's purpose; your purpose is unique to you. It's an expression of who you are and why you do what you do. Your Unguarded Moments will play a vital part in helping you find the clarity you need to grasp and define your purpose theme in a way that's both inspiring and practical.

Understanding purpose is humanity's age-old quest. The five archetypes above helped me narrow down my own search for meaning; I know they will help you as well. Chances are, you had an 'a-ha!' about your purpose just reading those.

I've found with my clients that identifying a purpose 'theme' helps accelerate the process of distilling a purpose statement. Once you have this piece in place, you can begin connecting your identity – your strengths, motivators, core values, and even personal stories – to this theme. Soon, you'll start to see a thread running through all of it.

For example, my purpose theme is Impact. My motivators are learning, teaching, and sharing. My strengths (according to the CliftonStrengths assessment) are Maximizer, Individualization, Strategy, Learner, and Achiever. And my core values are integrity, excellence, equality, freedom, fairness, and karma.

My purpose theme shows me that I find fulfilment from impacting and influencing others. My motivators show me that through shared experiences, I can create inspiration. My strengths indicate my belief that all individuals can achieve greatness. And my values centre on fostering perpetual growth and improvement in myself and others. When I put it all together, it's clear that my path is to impact others and inspire their greatness through teaching, relationships, and 'walking my talk'.

Looking back, it's easy to see the threads that tie it all together. But the truth is, it took me nearly a year to go through the process of selecting my purpose. I began with the self-discovery processes we discussed in Chapter 3, then I selected my purpose theme. Every couple of weeks, I would incorporate a new thought or idea, and put it into action, asking, 'If this is my purpose, how can I express it today?' After about 90 days, this process started having a significant impact in multiple areas of my life.

When you become clear on both your values and your category of purpose, you will begin to feel an inner solidity. You will start to notice when your everyday decisions aren't aligned with your values and purpose and correct them in the moment. You will begin to make intentional choices and create better boundaries around those choices. And, most of all, those you lead will start to see a level of authenticity and consistency from you that may not have been present before.

It's also important to know that you can bring your purpose into everything you do, no matter where you work, who you work with, or where you are in your leadership journey. You might work for an organization that has no defined purpose; you can create meaning in your work by incorporating your personal purpose into your daily tasks. You might work for an organization that has a purpose that's different to yours. If so, try to find ways to align your personal purpose with that of your company. If you can't, consider making a move to a new department or company so you can leverage your purpose and Intentional Leadership to the fullest.

You may have heard the adage, 'If you do what you love, you will never work a day in your life.' I think that's rubbish; work is work, and sometimes it's less fun than we'd like. However, if you *live your purpose* every day, you will always feel fulfilled and have the energy to go forwards, even through the toughest challenges.

Purpose within organizations

Every leader needs to be clear on their core values and purpose to respond in the most intentional way possible to everyday problems and challenges. Additionally, organizations also have their own value systems, and can express purpose in much the same way as individuals.

Purpose is generally expressed at an organizational level through a 'purpose statement'. Here are a few great ones:

- 3M: to solve unsolved problems innovatively;
- Mary Kay Cosmetics: to give unlimited opportunity to women;
- Walt Disney: to make people happy.

A company's purpose is its 'what for' – its reason for being in business. A compelling purpose can be tapped by employees and leadership to create idealistic as well as financial motivations for doing the company's work.

A company's purpose can be seen as much in what it chooses *not* to do as in what it does. For example, CVS decided to stop selling tobacco products in its stores in 2014 because smoking is in direct contradiction to CVS's purpose – perpetuating health and wellness. Southwest Airlines' purpose is 'Connect People to what's important in their lives through friendly, reliable, and low-cost air travel.' To this end, they don't charge passengers for the first two checked bags, even on bargain flights. Zappos, a company built on superior customer service whose purpose is 'to live and deliver WOW!' doesn't track call times for representatives, so there's no pressure on operators to resolve issues before the customer is fully satisfied.

At Atrion, our core purpose statement was 'Positively impacting the lives of others.' A lot of people thought this was incongruent for an IT services company. After all, how could a tech company make a difference in people's lives? But we were committed to it, and worked towards it every day. We looked at all of our contracts and clients, and asked, 'How can we find purpose in that?' And we regularly shared stories with our employees of how their work positively impacted the lives of our employees, our clients, and the community at large.

For example, one of our clients manufactured a heart monitor that was installed in ambulances. This monitor used the latest technology to send telemetry information for cardiac patients to the hospital en route. Hospitals could then assess patients' needs before they arrived and have the most appropriate emergency treatment prepared as soon as the ambulance pulled up to the emergency unit doors.

To the people working in our call centre, the reality of this life-saving technology seemed distant. After all, they were just taking calls and troubleshooting network issues. But one day, one of our employees had a heart attack at his desk. Between one breath and the next, he collapsed on the floor.

Our team sprang into action. They called 9-1-1, delivered CPR, and followed the emergency response procedures to the letter. When the ambulance arrived, the emergency medical technicians hooked our employee up to the same telemetry equipment we'd been supporting for years. He was wheeled into the operating room just 21 minutes after he collapsed, because the hospital staff had the diagnostic information – transmitted through the technology we supported – that they needed to save his life.

A clear expression of purpose helps people in your organization who are doing even mundane, repetitive jobs see value in what they accomplish every day. Our call centre staff weren't troubleshooting network issues. They were monitoring and maintaining life-saving technology that directly impacted our community. In that sense, Atrion wasn't a technology company. We were a life-saving company. Being able to clearly communicate that dramatically increased employee engagement, productivity, and satisfaction – and all of this was passed on to our clients.

Too often, companies fail to draw a clear line between purpose and action. If a stated purpose isn't backed up with strong core values, it feels flimsy. If we post our purpose statement on our website but don't prop it up with discussion, action, and clear decision-making throughout the organization, employees disengage, lose interest, and feel unappreciated. And if we aren't willing to prioritize our values above short-term gains, or otherwise sacrifice to defend them, our purpose becomes meaningless. When any (or all) of these things happen, the company as a whole slips into Ghost Mode.

It isn't the responsibility of individual employees to find purpose in what an organization does. While a few will be energized by their individual purpose – particularly those who fall into the purpose category of Achievement and/or who tend to be natural 'climbers' – most need guidance to make the connection between their daily tasks and the greater good. It's the job of Intentional Leaders to forge this link and keep it strong, so that everyone remains excited, engaged, and empowered.

Ask yourself: how much more invested would your team be if, instead of working towards some numerical quarterly goal, you were collectively working to bring greater innovation, joy, or efficiency to the world? And what if you could attract and hire new team members not just based on their skillsets, but on shared values and purpose?

Vision: the manifestation of your ideology

Many people confuse purpose with vision. However, they are very different.

Purpose, as we learned earlier, is why you do what you do – the deeper meaning in the work you and your team perform. It's how you express your values, regardless of what actual tasks you are doing. *Vision* is your aspirational goal for growth. It is given direction and trajectory by your values and purpose; it's what you intend to *do* with your purpose.

Vision is both tangible and forward-looking. It's the end game, the far horizon. You probably won't ever achieve it, but you can continuously move closer to it. If you keep it in your sights at all times, your vision will tell you where you are veering off track, making unnecessary detours, or getting turned around entirely.

Vision is also different from goals. Goals are the mile markers that show you where you're making progress. They have a finite endpoint; you either complete them, or you don't. They're essential, but they only represent a piece of the big picture.

For example, your vision might be to create a world where everyone is connected by technology. Your goal (which moves you closer to that vision) might be to sell two million smartphones in the first quarter of your business year. You will strive to meet that quota, but your vision isn't complete when the goal is met.

We can and should create a clear vision for ourselves on an individual level, as well as for our organizations. Both need to be considered when we are making intentional choices as leaders. And while they don't need to be identical, our individual and organizational visions need to have at least some overlap if we are to make an impact as leaders.

Some of the clearest examples of how vision propels an organization forwards can be found in the non-profit world. The dedicated employees and volunteers at my client, College Crusades, demonstrate how a clear vision – underpinned by purpose – can help everyone do their best work.

College Crusades' purpose is to allow every Rhode Island youth to participate in the American Dream in their own way. Their vision is to empower all students in Rhode Island – particularly those in economically challenged areas – to complete a post-secondary-school or college programme, so they can flourish and contribute to their communities. Their goal each school year might be to enrol a certain number of students into their programmes or increase those students' school participation by a certain percentile – but while the goals may change, the end game never does.

With this level of clarity, everyone who works for College Crusades knows exactly what impact they are having and what outcome they want to create: more first-generation students attending college. They don't get lost in the daily grind or wonder what the point of their tasks is. Every programme, activity, tutoring session, and conversation is strengthened by the knowledge that they are contributing to the lifetime success and well-being of their students – most of whom are first-generation Americans and the first in their families to go to college. The impact of their programmes, and the amazing success of their students, is well documented and woven into the daily narrative, so it's always present.

But while a clear vision may be commonplace in the non-profit world, it tends to get cloudy in the for-profit sector. Many companies don't have a clear vision beyond 'make a profit and continually improve our products'. The issue with a weak vision (as with a weak or undefined purpose) is that it's hard for employees and leaders to connect to, leverage, and incorporate into daily tasks.

In his famous 'I Have a Dream' speech, Dr Martin Luther King, Jr outlined a clear vision for his life and work: to create a world where people were judged not by the colour of their skin, but by the content of their character; and where the children of slaves and slave owners could sit at one table, together.

Everything that King did until the day of his assassination was in pursuit of that vision. The speeches he gave, the opportunities he cultivated, the relationships he forged: all of them were aligned with that aspirational vision. His vision was so clear, and so compelling, that he drew powerful and enduring support to his cause – support that continues nearly 60 years after that speech was delivered.

Your personal vision: what's your lifelong theme?

Not everyone has a vision to change the world – and that's OK! But chances are, you have a vision for your life, even if you haven't fully defined it yet. It's the way you want to leave the world better than you found it. It's the way you want to make others feel. It's the way *you* want to feel overall.

Glenn Clark was a client and a personal friend. After our first meeting in 1992, I noticed that he shared one of my favourite Emerson quotes in his email signature. The next time we talked, we started sharing our Core Ideologies.

Glenn's purpose was love. His vision was to leave the world a better place than he found it every day of his life. When he passed away from pancreatic cancer at the age of 51, he was memorialized by hundreds of friends, all of whom had a story to share about how Glenn made their lives better. He lived his Core Ideology more truly than anyone I've ever known.

I encourage every leader I work with to schedule a few hours to create a personal vision for themselves. The power we have to make a lasting impact through this work cannot be overstated. If you're not sure where to start, try looking for a theme. Consider your proudest moments. Your biggest accomplishments. Your happiest times. What do they all have in common?

Your organization's vision: what are you working for, and why?

It's sad that many companies spend more time wordsmithing their values, purpose, and vision statements for public consumption than they do actually embodying them. This isn't to say that you shouldn't make your organization's Core Ideology public. Your customers absolutely should know your values. Even more than the products you sell or services you offer, your values are how you will connect with your customers and clients most deeply. When values overlap, connections are forged. But in the end, what matters to your customers is what you're doing *right now*. What matters to your employees, on the other hand, is where you are going and what you stand for.

It's vital for your employees to understand and connect with your company's vision, because, even more than purpose, it helps them feel like they're part of something bigger than themselves. Remember, your vision is the ultimate destination, the long game.

At Atrion, our vision was 'To be the top 1 per cent of our industry.' One of the ways we communicated this was to say, 'We want to become the Harvard Business School of our industry. Wouldn't it be great if, no matter where you went in the world, Atrion always topped the list of "The Best Tech Companies to Work With?"' This vision set the stage for excellence in all areas of what we did – but also allowed us to become exclusive about whom we hired, and whom we took on as clients. If we wanted to be the Harvard of the IT world, we couldn't run our day-to-day operations by community-college standards. Our vision helped us make discerning choices even when maintaining the status quo, or replicating what the competition was doing, was more comfortable.

Your Core Ideology is the foundation of trust

Great leaders make the choices others won't. That's why they create the results others can't.

When times are uncertain, we look to great leaders to show us the way – just as our teams look to us. But what happens when leadership isn't supported by a strong Core Ideology?

The answer is simple: trust breaks down. Leaders and organizations that don't have a defined and accessible Core Ideology don't inspire trust in others because there is no clear barometer for their decisions. If we as leaders make choices based on a changeable or conditional set of criteria – like permission-to-play or accidental values – our teams, clients, and customers will never know where they stand with us. In essence, we're saying, 'Trust me', without giving any clear indication that we are trustworthy.

Operating according to a clear Core Ideology provides a foundation of consistency for everyone around us. We become more reliable, more predictable. More deserving of trust. And, perhaps more importantly, we begin to trust ourselves.

Self-trust is the hallmark of inner authority. When we trust ourselves to make the best possible decisions (in alignment with our values, purpose, and vision) using whatever information and resources are available to us, we feel more confident. We can follow our instincts, 'go with the gut'. We know that where we want to go might require us to walk a different path – and instead of asking 'Am I wrong?' we start asking, 'How do I get there?' Inspiration, innovation, and radical growth all begin with self-trust.

When we trust ourselves, we inspire trust in others. And where there is trust, it's easier to move people forwards. As Stephen Covey explores in his book *The Speed of Trust*, the speed at which trust is established is critical to the success of both individuals and organizations.

Remember, trust is the primary rope we're towing as leaders. And trust requires clarity.

Clarity creates certainty. It's how we as Intentional Leaders lead from the front of the line. Clarity is created when we provide concrete information about where we're going (vision), why we're going there (purpose) and how we intend to get there (values). When obstacles do come up, a shared Core Ideology helps everyone holding the line change direction together.

Trust is the currency of leadership. If I don't know and trust myself as a leader, I'm stumbling around at the front of the line, bumping up against obstacles, taking wrong turns, and basically dragging everyone around in circles. And the more obvious it becomes that I don't have a clear destination, the less everyone wants to follow me. I'm in Ghost Mode, reacting to every little thing on the surface without understanding the deeper current.

On the other hand, if I am clear on my Core Ideology, I can get out in front and call people forwards. They will get excited about what we're doing and where we're going. They'll be compelled to engage and carry their own weight. I may even feel like they're helping to push me forwards. This is what people refer to as 'momentum'.

* * *

As you can see, Core Ideology is far more than just words on paper. It's an individualized, ethically-sound, deep-current approach to building a foundation for intentional leadership.

As Joe Batten wrote, 'Our value is the sum of our values.' When you know what you stand for, you will also come to fully understand your value to your team, your organization, the world – and most importantly, to yourself.

Reflection

- Your Core Ideology consists of these foundational elements: your *core values*, which are the *foundation* of your ideology; your *purpose*, which is the *expression* of your ideology; and your *vision*, which is the *manifestation* of your ideology.
- A strong Core Ideology is the foundation of trust. Trust is the currency of leadership.

- A clear Core Ideology gets people excited about what you're doing and where you're going.
- Your purpose is to perpetuate the things you value. A company's purpose is its reason for being in business. An effective purpose can be tapped by employees and leadership to create idealistic as well as financial motivations for doing the company's work.
- Many people confuse purpose with vision. However, they are very different. Purpose is how you express your values, regardless of what actual tasks you are doing. Vision is your aspirational goal for growth which is given direction and trajectory by your values and purpose; it's what you intend to *do* with your purpose.

Unity of Thought and Action

Thought – how strong is your inner authority?

When we identify and define what we stand for, and allow that truth to guide our decision-making and actions, we establish inner authority – a deep, well-founded trust in ourselves. Based on this thought, do you feel you have a strong Core Ideology and inner authority? How much do you trust yourself as a leader?

Action – create your Core Ideology

Create several Unguarded Moments this week to engage with your Core Ideology. Identify and clarify your values, purpose, and vision. Write out statements for each so you can begin to pull your Core Ideology into your daily decision-making.

CHAPTER 5

Ego: Finding Balance Between Self and Others

'Good men must not obey the laws too well.' – Emerson

Josh was a super-talented freelancer who made a name for himself doing small gigs leading complex, technical projects. Eventually, he was hired by an IT services company in California as a Microsoft practice lead, where he quickly outshone everyone in his department. Within a year, he got promoted and found himself in charge of the ten-person team he'd been part of only days before.

Josh's buddy-to-boss transition was the first of his career, and he felt it was the next logical step. While there were plenty of people who'd been working there years longer than him, everyone agreed, 'It couldn't have happened to a nicer guy.'

Josh was the kind of guy *everyone* liked. He was technically talented, friendly, easy to talk to, and would go miles out of his way for anyone on his team. But what no one realized (including Josh himself) was that Josh did these things out of a deep need to be liked and included. He said 'Yes!' to everything because he was afraid that others would shut him out if he said no.

Being a people pleaser worked well for Josh when he was an individual contributor, but it completely undermined him as a manager. He was passive in challenging leadership situations, and often told people what they wanted to hear instead of what needed to be said. His strategy for dealing with difficult team members was to ignore the problem and hope it went away. He was more concerned with staying in his team's good books than he was with leading them in the direction of their goals.

Difficult conversations with team members were put off almost indefinitely – or until they could no longer be ignored. Problems that could have been resolved in moments went on for months. Some people on Josh's team were independent and self-motivated; these individuals loved working under him because he didn't micromanage. But those who needed collaboration and direction became more and more discontented, and their output dropped. Things came to a head when, after five consecutive meetings with one employee (during which he told her all the things she was doing right, but never touched on the issue at hand), he finally came to the point and told her what needed to change.

'So, you're telling me that my job is in jeopardy, now? What were all the rest of our conversations about?' the employee snapped. 'I thought that I was doing good, and now, I'm learning that you're disappointed in my work. What am I missing?'

Josh's all-carrot-and-no-stick strategy had backfired in his face. He called me that night, deeply upset. 'I don't know what I'm doing wrong!' he confessed. 'I try to let everyone just do their thing, but these issues keep getting worse.'

'Josh,' I said, 'your team doesn't want a friend. They want a leader. They can't get results if they don't know what you expect of them. Those hard conversations are necessary. They need to happen in a way that resolves issues quickly and invites everyone to do better. And you have to find a way not to obsess about how people are going to react to your feedback, so you can spend more time planning how you're going to steer the conversation.'

I mentored Josh for several months as he found his way in his new leadership role. Contrary to what he'd initially believed, when he addressed issues quickly and without drama, his team respected him more. And when he reflected on the reasons why he'd been locked into being the 'nice guy', he realized that he needed to build up his self-confidence from within, rather than look for outside validation. As he practised self-awareness, examined his values, and began to strengthen his inner authority, he could extend more trust to his team, even in challenging situations.

Two years after he first called me, Josh's team had become the highest producing in the company. He was being considered for the company's recently vacated chief technology officer position. Josh felt that he was ready to tackle this next big step in his career. His ability to lead intentionally and be more assertive in difficult situations had had a significant impact on the organization's success.

The day he called to tell me he'd got the job, Josh said, 'You know, it was the coolest thing. When I got the promotion, my team took me to lunch, and they talked about how much I've grown as a leader. A couple joked that they'd had bets that I would not last six months. At the end of lunch, Amy – you know, the one who stormed out of my office after our first difficult conversation – dropped by to give me a card. She wrote, "I'm so happy for you. This company is going to be even better with you as its CTO. Thanks for being such a great guy." I couldn't believe it.'

A Healthy ego supports Intentional Leadership

Every one of us has an ego. It's part of being a human.

The Merriam-Webster dictionary defines ego as:

1. The self, especially as contrasted with another self or the world, and
2. The one of the three divisions of the psyche in psychoanalytic theory that serves as the organized conscious mediator between the person and reality, especially by functioning both in the perception of and adaptation to reality.

In Latin, *ego* means 'I'. Without 'I', there can be no 'you'. Without a healthy ego, there can be no awareness of oneself as a human being. Many spiritual traditions and pop psychology books make ego out to be a bad thing – something we need to overcome or cancel out. However, the reality is that we *need* our ego to strike a balance between our inner authority and our outer experiences, circumstances, and relationships. We don't need to erase the ego; we just need to become aware of it, and then adjust, tune, and calibrate it properly so that we can show up exactly how we're needed in crucial situations.

As I shared in Chapter 2, I see ego as a spectrum – like an audio display on a stereo. It can be whisper-quiet, or loud enough to shake the walls. Most of us have a general range in which we operate – but we are most healthy as leaders when our egos are in the middle range. This balances our inner authority with our desire to connect with and get along with others.

When our ego is too 'low' or underdeveloped, it's like we have the volume turned down on our inner authority. We have low self-esteem. We engage in people-pleasing behaviours, and let others' opinions dictate or influence our actions. We make what others think more important than what we know. We question or backtrack on our decisions, procrastinate, live in fear of making mistakes, and avoid confrontation like the plague. Most of all, we go with the flow when we should be taking a stand – even when that flow is in opposition to our values, instincts, and knowledge.

Josh, in our story above, was in Ghost Mode, leading with an underdeveloped ego. Instead of being present to the reality of the situation and leading intentionally, he did everything he could to ignore the problem. None of this was malicious, but it was still causing him and his team a lot of unnecessary stress.

Because his ego was underdeveloped, Josh didn't believe in himself. He avoided challenging conversations. He went with the flow even when it didn't serve him or his team. And every time things went wrong, it confirmed his self-belief that he didn't know what he was doing. And the more he did the same things, the louder the stories in his head became. It was a vicious cycle – and it was keeping him in Ghost Mode.

To come into balance in his new role and become an Intentional Leader, Josh didn't need to be nicer, more approachable, or more giving. He didn't need to be a better listener or learn new body language techniques to set others at ease. He didn't need to get better at people pleasing. Instead, he needed to practise awareness, turn *up* the dial on his ego, and find a way to trust himself even when his biggest fear – not being liked – was staring him in the face.

Josh didn't need strategies and techniques on how to have crucial conversations. He needed to become more present to who he was as a person and a leader, find some stable ground around his values, and strengthen his underdeveloped ego. Once there, he could start to trust himself more, and stop letting other people's feelings about him dictate his actions. He could also empower his team to believe in themselves and rely on their own inner authority – just as he was learning to rely on his.

The result? Josh became an Intentional Leader, not just a nice guy sitting behind a manager's desk.

On the other side of the spectrum, of course, is an overdeveloped ego. At the extreme edge of this range are those we might describe as self-absorbed, overconfident, lacking in compassion or narcissistic. However, this place isn't reserved for the 'egomaniacs' alone; many of us can slip into it for short periods without noticing. When we're in this state, we listen to our authority above all else. We minimize other people and leverage relationships for personal gain – except when something goes wrong, in which case we blame everyone else for messing things up for us. We tell stories to ourselves and others about why we're unconditionally right, and others are wrong. In other words, we have our ego 'volume' turned up so high that we can't hear what's going on outside our heads.

Take Thurston, for instance, the COO of a company that engaged me to lead an internal leadership development programme. Thurston was *never* wrong. Even when confronted with overwhelming evidence to the contrary, he wouldn't admit to making a mistake. When things went well, he put on a great face, and could be generous with his time and compliments. But when things went poorly, everyone started covering their butts because they knew he'd be looking for a scapegoat and finding ways to assign blame. After all, it couldn't possibly be *his* fault things had gone south.

Everything his team did needed to be approved, personally, by him – right down to $25 supply purchases. If a team member left an email unanswered for more than a few minutes, he took it as a personal affront. But it wasn't uncommon for the same team member to waste days waiting on his approval to move forwards with a critical task. As a result, his team was completely disempowered. They lived in fear of his temper, and often skirted around pressing issues in meetings because 'it just isn't worth the blowout'. When eruptions did happen, the team was conditioned to 'throw him the red meat' – meaning they would intentionally find something or someone to blame to shift his aggression away from them.

Thurston's actions and behaviours created a culture that punished accountability and lacked empowerment. His team spent more time pointing fingers, shifting blame, and justifying their choices than they did on activities that would improve performance. Sure, they used words like 'accountability', 'ownership', and 'responsibility' in meetings, but those values were never implemented.

This toxic situation was made worse by the fact that Thurston spoke negatively about his team as a whole. He regularly disparaged individual team members in front of fellow employees and even customers. In many cases, he would share with people outside the organization that he planned to fire someone – and as a result, that unfortunate employee would linger in dread for days or weeks before he pulled the trigger.

Thurston was operating in an unhealthy spectrum of ego. The polar opposite of Josh, he didn't appear to care a bit if his team liked him. What mattered was that they obeyed and feared him. He expected them to do whatever he said, because 'only he knew how to handle things around here'. And if someone had the audacity to draw the line regarding his toxic management style (or worse, offer their two weeks' notice), he ignored them until they went away. No conversations, no goodbyes.

When I approached Thurston about potential new ways to handle an issue with his team, he brushed me off. 'I didn't hire you to lecture *me*,' he said. 'I hired you to teach those guys how to do a better job.'

Needless to say, I spent the rest of my contract helping that company's middle management learn to navigate in the wake of an egomaniac.

By this point, I'm sure you understand the need to develop a strong inner authority and the awareness necessary to balance your ego. While most of us aren't egomaniacs, many of us slip into this 'too-loud' ego state from time to time when we get too confident, too complacent or tell ourselves that we are irreplaceable. Self-awareness helps us quickly dial the volume down to a healthy level.

Other times, we find ourselves in Josh's position, with our ego's volume turned down so low that we lose faith in ourselves and our capabilities. We tell ourselves that we don't matter, or that we can never work hard enough to make a difference. Self-awareness also helps us navigate these moments and reconnect to our inner authority and self-trust.

What may surprise you is that, at the end of the day, Thurston's results and Josh's results were *almost the same*. Both got things done. Both (for the most part) met expectations, revenue goals, and deadlines. Yet, both were operating in Ghost Mode in an unhealthy spectrum of ego. As a result, critical conversations were avoided. Forward momentum was slowed. Trust was undermined. Neither they nor their teams were fully empowered to do their best work – and so their success in the long term was undermined.

Healthy ego = empowerment for everyone

Self-reflection and self-awareness – getting to know who we are – supports the development of inner authority, which in turn creates a strong and healthy ego. We come to understand that, as leaders, we have a responsibility to hold the space for our teams in accordance with our goals, our values, and our purpose. We create congruence between our thoughts, words, and behaviours. We build trust in ourselves so we can hold our ground during challenging conversations and situations. And we become humble enough to learn where our challenges lie and do what it takes to correct them.

However, a healthy ego impacts more than just our inner authority and self-trust. It amplifies our leadership capabilities because it allows us to dial our ego up or down to meet the needs of any situation. For example, in a crisis situation, we might turn up our ego to be more decisive and minimize the 'noise' of others' panic and uncertainty. Conversely, when an employee approaches us for a private conversation, we can quiet our ego to hear and relate more clearly.

But perhaps the greatest gift of a healthy ego is that *it frees us from perceiving others' success as a threat.* We know who we are, and accept both our strengths and our shortcomings. This allows us to extend greater trust, accept support from others whose strengths complement our own, and build inclusive momentum for our entire team through our shared Core Ideology.

Empowerment can mean different things to different people. Our relationship to the word largely depends on our experiences, circumstances, aspirations, and even our upbringing. However, for our purposes here, I want you to think of 'empowerment' not as a concept, but as a process.

Empowerment in leadership consists of three crucial components: autonomy, authority, and influence. When we empower others, we allow them to operate with autonomy – meaning they have control over how they do their job. We give them the authority to make decisions within established parameters (which reinforces their sense of freedom and autonomy). And we allow their ideas, actions, and attitudes to influence the outcome of the project.

When we are at the unhealthy ends of the ego spectrum, others' talents, progress, or successes can feel threatening and trigger a state of cognitive dissonance. We feel that we might be displaced or invalidated by what others are achieving. In this state, we tend to disempower others to lessen the feeling of threat to ourselves.

Both Josh and Thurston created this kind of disempowerment among their team members. They were trying to control what we can never control: the thoughts, feelings, and actions of other people. The reasons for this desire for control were very different – but, as we explored earlier, the effect was essentially the same.

It's more common than you'd think for employees to cater to or manage a leader's unhealthy ego. You can probably call up more than one example from your own career without thinking too hard about it. But here's the thing: *it is no one's job but yours to manage, maintain, or protect your sense of self.*

In other words: your ego, your problem.

Walking the empowerment tightrope

Empowerment is a tricky concept for many leaders because it requires a delicate balance. On the one hand, it means setting clear boundaries for your team and holding them accountable to your shared goals and vision. On the other hand, it means letting go of some portion of control so that everyone can shine in his or her role.

In my early days at Atrion, I took a lot of pride in being the most technical person in our company. It became part of my identity. When our rapid growth required me to take on a more executive role, I hired a guy who was even smarter and more technical than I was to take over my old duties. On the one hand, it felt like a victory, because obviously he would be an asset to Atrion. On the other hand, I felt threatened. There were moments when I was tempted to micromanage my new hire just to maintain my sense of relevance.

The truth was, my insecurity had nothing to do with the new guy (whose name was, let's say, Daniel) but with the challenge my new executive role was presenting to my ego. In order to step into my new role, I had to let go of the work that had defined me since I was 17. I had to move from a space where I always knew the answer to one where I faced a steep learning curve. Most of all, I needed to acknowledge that Daniel was, in fact, the perfect person for the job. He always rose to the occasion, and never let me down.

Thankfully, I had already gained some of the tools to be able to observe this behaviour in myself, and I was able to rein in my reaction before I caused too much damage. The only way out of my discomfort was to believe that I had what it took to become a good executive and leader, and trust myself to learn the ropes. I couldn't empower Daniel to succeed without first empowering myself.

I can't do my best work as a leader if I'm living in fear of what others think of me, shying away from challenges or trying to make everyone happy all the time. Nor can I do it if I'm putting others down, convinced that I have nothing to learn, or refusing to let go of my chosen tasks and responsibilities.

My ego, my problem.

When we practise presence and build our sense of inner authority, we develop a level of awareness that naturally brings our ego into greater balance. We know where our greatest strengths and competences are, and where we are less competent; this shows us where and how to ask for support to execute our vision. Trusting ourselves empowers us to trust others.

As Intentional Leaders, our biggest job isn't to create revenue or results, although those are important. It's to empower the people around us to do their best work, create their best lives, and be their best selves; when this happens, revenue and results follow.

So why don't more leaders do this naturally? It has to do with mindset.

Empowerment requires a growth mindset

Before her promotion to a leadership role, Karen had been a high-impact individual contributor in her company. She loved her work and took pride in the quality of what she produced. Everyone in the organization could count on her to deliver the goods, and her talents were highly respected.

However, in her new position, she quickly became overwhelmed. She was working 80-plus hours a week, but still couldn't keep up.

'I need some guidance about how to delegate,' she told me.

After several sessions, we identified tasks that she could pass on to her team. We also strategized about how she could empower her team to take on these new responsibilities.

Eventually, the big day came: Karen sat down with a key employee to assign her a new task. They had a fantastic conversation, and the employee was excited about taking on the new responsibility.

At our next session, I asked Karen to walk me through the meeting. After explaining the details of the conversation, she said, 'Last night I had a stroke of genius. I decided to create a procedural document and give it to the employee so she will do this right.' I asked to see the procedural. It was a beautifully constructed and highly detailed 12-page document complete with screenshots, arrows, and sidebars. It was, in Karen's words, 'idiot-proof'.

'What happens if the employee swaps Steps 4 and 5?' I asked.

Karen blew a gasket. She made it very clear that there would be no deviation from the procedure she'd created. This was *the only way* it could be done.

We had several conversations about the difference between delegation and empowerment. Karen soon realized that her document was helpful for training purposes, but wasn't empowering for her employee in the long term because it didn't allow her to own the work.

Luckily, Karen was open to this feedback, and exhibited what has come to be known in leadership circles as a 'growth mindset'. Popularized by Carol Dweck, a growth mindset is the belief that our most basic abilities can be developed through hard work, dedication, and an unwavering passion for learning. Karen's growth mindset meant that, although she had worked hard on her procedural, she was willing to harness her ego and change her approach to achieve a better result.

Her new formula for delegation was less task-oriented and far more empowering. She prepared her team through discussion to take on new responsibilities. Next, she trained them on the tools, processes, and reasoning for each step. Finally, she asked *them* to create a documented procedural, which she would review. She trusted them with the responsibility, and was rewarded with their ownership.

And in the end, if they decided to swap Step 4 for Step 5, she was willing to let it go – as long as it didn't impact the outcome of the work.

Why don't we empower others?

When you're a hard-working, results-producing individual contributor like Karen, you are more likely than others to get a promotion to a leadership role. However, as both she and Josh learned (and as I learned as well), the very skills that make you a great individual contributor can hold you back in a leadership role.

When we don't empower others, the cause is almost always an unbalanced ego. However, the symptoms may be one or more of the following:

- Fear
  - fear of letting go;
  - fear of losing control;
  - fear of losing part of our identity.
- Perception/assumption
  - belief that others aren't capable, equipped or ready to do the tasks;
  - belief that others should 'just know what to do';
  - belief that we can do it better;
  - belief that we are indispensable or irreplaceable.
- Time
  - belief that we don't have time to teach others to do the task properly;
  - lacking patience to teach others.

- Boundaries
  - belief that teaching/empowering is not within the scope of our role;
  - belief that delegation will impact consistency.

Let me be clear: all of these are excuses. As Intentional Leaders, *our most vital role is to empower.* No aspect of the empowerment process falls outside our job description. That means that it's also part of our job to root out the excuses we use to avoid empowering others.

The first skill we must master with regard to empowerment is ego management. The second is a growth mindset.

Some people are naturally excited about learning. They can't wait to gather and apply new information so that they can grow personally and professionally. They fully believe that they can learn whatever information, skills, or behaviours they need to succeed – and that, when challenges arise, all they need to do is keep trying.

Others believe that talent is given at birth; either people are good at things or they aren't, and no amount of practice or trying will change that. This can result in a sense of powerlessness, victimhood, or fatalism – or, it can create a belief that no one else can do what we do, and we have nothing to learn from others.

The first way of thinking is called a 'growth mindset'. The second is a 'fixed mindset'. Interestingly, they correspond precisely to the spectrum of healthy versus unhealthy ego.

When our ego is healthy, we have a firm footing in who we are through our inner authority and clear Core Ideology. We have the compass of our values to guide us, and we trust ourselves to make better decisions. At the same time, we don't allow our inability to do something define who we are. Instead, we trust ourselves to learn whatever is necessary to create the best possible outcome.

On the other hand, when our ego is unhealthy, every learning curve feels like a threat. If we need to learn, it must be because, somehow, *we* are wrong. For an underdeveloped ego, this can trigger self-doubt, shame or a sense of being victimized by others or the situation. 'If only I was [insert quality here],' the underdeveloped ego says, 'this wouldn't be happening.' For an overdeveloped ego, the feeling of 'being wrong' is the same, but the response is different: instead of retreating into self-doubt, we rationalize our 'rightness' and make others or the situation wrong instead.

When we're in a fixed mindset (on either extreme of the ego spectrum), there's a drive to hide our flaws and mistakes, rather than seeing them as opportunities for learning and growth.

When we, as Intentional Leaders, adopt a growth mindset, we take a lot of the pressure off ourselves. We can learn and grow without making the learning and growing a judgement about who we are. We no longer need to rationalize or justify our behaviours; instead, we are willing to adapt.

There is no right or wrong way to be a leader, just as there is no right or wrong way to be a human. However, there are *effective* and *ineffective* ways to show up as a leader. Effective leaders lead from a healthy level of ego, using the platform of their values, purpose, and vision. But to make that adjustment, we need the flexibility of a growth mindset.

The easiest way to recognize where you've slipped into a fixed mindset is to ask, 'Am I seeing this person, task, or moment as a problem or an opportunity?' If it's the former, you're in a fixed mindset. So how do you get unstuck? Through Unguarded Moments, of course! Spend time sitting with your self-awareness. Get curious about your strengths and weaknesses. Be willing to let the truth about who you are come through, even if it's uncomfortable. Where are you excited to grow, and where are you deploying excuses?

Once you've achieved clarity about where growth needs to happen, spend some time redefining failure. Look at what your past mistakes have taught you, and be willing to accept and integrate what you have learned. Then, you can embrace challenges instead of avoiding them.

Finally, I'd like you to consider how and when you're learning. We've all heard the proverb, 'Necessity is the mother of invention.' However, it's vital to recognize the difference between necessity and fear. Learning out of passion and a desire to expand creates growth – i.e., 'I need to learn this in order to reach my goal.' However, when you try to learn out of fear of failure or the pressure to 'fix' something, contraction and frustration occur. Use your Unguarded Moments to determine why and how you will undertake a new learning curve so you can better manage your ego and feed your growth mindset.

Out the window or in the mirror?

In his book *Good to Great*, Jim Collins writes about the 'Window and Mirror' leadership model, which corresponds closely to the idea of fixed and growth mindsets. The concept is simple: as a leader, when do you look out of the window at everyone else, and when do you look in the mirror?

According to Collins, exemplary leaders look out of the window when things are going well, saying, 'Look what we've accomplished together!' But when things go wrong, the first place they look is in the mirror. They ask, 'How do I need to improve so we can all get better results next time?' This is an indication of a growth mindset and a healthy ego.

On the other hand, leaders with fixed mindsets and/or unhealthy egos look in the mirror when things are going great and say, 'Look what I've accomplished!' But when things don't go so well, they look out of the window and blame everyone else for messing up.

A perfect example of these extremes of leadership can be found in America's favourite pastime, football. I'm a huge Patriots fan. Part of it is that I'm a native New Englander, and being a Pats fan is pretty much a prerequisite from birth. The memories of the Pats' less-than-stellar years still hurt; I remember the futility of the 3-and-13 seasons and the 1-and-15 travesties. But over the last two decades, my fascination with the Patriots leadership model has grown beyond wins and losses.

Bill Belichick and his coaches operate from the certainty that, to play their best game, they need to trust and empower every one of their players – and that each player needs to trust and empower himself. Simply stated, this means 'Do your job!' In practice, this looks like keeping everyone's ego in a healthy place on the spectrum so that everyone remains confident and excited about learning. The entire team operates within a growth mindset. The expectation is for the position, not the player. That's why the Pats have been able to take cast-off players and turn them into champions – and why they survived the loss of star quarterback Tom Brady to injury.

Of course, the cut-throat world of professional football isn't a direct parallel to the average workplace. In football, an entire year of work is summarized in a few games; it's expected that each player is performing at his best, all the time. If that isn't the case, you can be dropped in a heartbeat. On the other hand, most employees are given time to develop their skills and grow into the role they've been assigned.

At the same time, the Patriot way has relevance to the workplace in two areas: the debrief model, and the sense of empowerment that comes from Intentional Leadership.

Other than intensive training, one of the key strategies the Pats employ is the debrief – the post-game look in the mirror. In that space, they talk about why decisions were made, what the results were, and what the impacts were. But most of all, they talk about where each of them were personally accountable. They hold up the mirror, and no one is exempt from looking in it. They're asked, 'What could you have done differently? What did you see here? What caused you to react in that way? Why were you in this position versus this position?' The person is then asked to analyse where, when, and why they were less effective than they could have been, so that everyone can do better next time.

Most businesses and individuals never do a debrief after a big win or loss. They either obsess over their failures or gloat over their successes, never considering how they might leverage either as a learning tool. The Patriots players don't have the luxury of 'letting it go'. I imagine it must be brutal sometimes to look objectively at a loss, especially when emotions are running high, but it's fair, and it's all oriented towards doing better when they get back out on to the field.

You can see this at play in many of former quarterback Tom Brady's post-game interviews. When they won, it was all about the team, and how everyone played their parts to the fullest. But when something went wrong – a play went poorly, there was an interception, etc. – Brady took full responsibility for his part in it. He didn't talk about how Edelman messed up when he failed to make the catch, or how the offensive line should have done a better job keeping people off his back. He didn't place blame. He only talked about his own mistakes, and how he planned to correct them in the future.

Bill Belichick also models this. He rarely singles out players for praise; it's always about the team. But when asked why the Pats lost a game or suffered a setback, his answer is usually some variation of, 'We were outcoached. That was on me.'

Compare that to other teams, who spend a lot of time and energy on blame. 'The quarterback did this, the running back did that, so I wasn't able to do my job.' And, of course, the people being blamed get defensive, and start telling their own stories about why they were the victims here, and how the other guy was the one who screwed up.

Bill Parcels, former head coach of both the Patriots and the New York Giants, was a prime example of this kind of leadership. Instead of reducing fixed mindset, he encouraged it. At press conferences, he'd throw people under the bus by name. In a stunning display of toxic masculinity, he would insult players by referring to them as 'she'. Yes, he still won games – including two Superbowls – but the Giants never had the sort of team solidarity that we see in the Patriots under Belichick, nor was their success so long-lived.

In the end, Belichick is the one wearing eight championship rings (six so far with the Patriots, and two as an assistant coach with the Giants). But he'd tell you that his teams did all the work. He's looking out of the window.

Nonconformity (aka, the road less travelled)

The combination of a healthy ego and a growth mindset allows us as leaders to do two crucial things. The first is to empower ourselves and our teams to continually learn, adapt, and outperform the standards we set for ourselves. The other is to take the road less travelled.

We've all heard that famous line from the poet Robert Frost: '*Two roads diverged in a wood, and I / I took the one less travelled by / And that has made all the difference.*'

As Intentional Leaders, the road to growth, innovation, and expansion often leads us into uncharted territory. When this happens, we have a choice: do what others have done before, or turn inwards and choose a road based on our values, purpose, and vision.

When we choose the road less travelled, there will be times when we get lost in the fog – when we can't be sure we're doing the right things, circumstances are shifting too fast to predict and everything feels uncertain.

During these times, we need to be able to rely on our inner authority. We need to trust that we are doing the right thing, even when we have no external evidence for it – and we need all the people who look to us for guidance to be able to trust in that as well.

9/11 was one of the first times I truly had to lean into my inner authority. We had no idea what the future had in store. It would have been easy to take the well-travelled path: cutting staff, pulling back, trying to outsmart the recession. Instead, we threw out the 'rules' and created a new model for survival. By thinking outside the box, we did what no one else in our industry was able to do: double in size during one of the worst economic periods in America's history.

Blazing new trails is one of the biggest joys and challenges of Intentional Leadership. We aren't bound to play by the rules; it's our job to *make* the rules, and set the example for how to navigate growth, uncertainty, and change. To do this successfully, we need to practise something that has been highly discouraged in the business world: *nonconformity.*

There's a big difference between nonconformity and rebellion. Nonconformity is the willingness to be different or deviate from the status quo in pursuit of a greater goal. Rebellion is the direct opposition to an institution or set of rules for the sake of diminishing or dismantling it. One is the result of trusting yourself; the other is a result of distrusting the system.

Walking the line between nonconformity and rebellion requires both trust in ourselves and transparency in our motivations. Before we ask others to follow us down that less-travelled road, we need to be clear about why we're going there and what we hope to achieve. Is change actually necessary, or do we want change for its own sake? Are we leading with a healthy ego to create greater empowerment, or rebelling from a place of unhealthy self-worth?

At the same time, we need to choose how much negative feedback and 'realism' we are willing to hear from those around us. Everything is impossible until someone does it; then, it's simply the way things are.

* * *

Bringing our ego into a healthy balance is one of the most powerful ways to combat Ghost Mode. In addition to gaining awareness of our behaviours, it empowers us to cultivate a growth mindset and change our relationship to challenges and circumstances. Instead of expecting the world to cater to us, we adapt to be what the world – and our vision – needs us to be.

If you recognized your own tendencies at either 'unhealthy' end of the ego spectrum, don't judge yourself. You are human – and therefore capable of growth and change. Use your Unguarded Moments, trust your inner authority, look in the mirror when you fail, and reach out for help when you need it. Soon, you will see your way clear to building a strong, healthy ego and empowering others to do and be their best.

A perfect visual for this work is a Lokai bracelet. At the top of the beaded circle is a white bead containing a drop of water from the top of Mount Everest. At the bottom is a black bead containing mud from the Dead Sea. The remaining beads that make up the bracelet are filled with clear water. The Lokai is a reminder to stay humble, even when you are on top of the world – and to remain hopeful when you hit a low point, because success will always come back around. It's a visual representation of the cycles of life and the spectrum of ego – and of the possibility inherent in being human.

Reflection

- Ego is a spectrum – like an audio display on a stereo. We are most healthy as leaders when our egos are in the middle range.
- Self-reflection and self-awareness – getting to know who we are – supports the development of inner authority, which in turn creates a strong and healthy ego.
- When we don't empower others, the cause is almost always an unbalanced ego. However, the symptoms may be one or more of the following: fear, perception/assumption, time, or boundaries. These are all excuses we make to avoid doing the work to empower others.
- As Intentional Leaders, the road to growth, innovation, and expansion often leads us into uncharted territory. When this happens, we have a choice: do what others have done before, or turn inwards and choose a road of *nonconformity* based on our values, purpose, and vision.

Unity of Thought and Action

Thought – how 'loud' are you being?

When our ego is healthy, we create trust. Trusting ourselves empowers us to trust others and empower them. What did the discussion of the ego spectrum bring up for you? Where do you think you are on the ego spectrum on a daily basis? How do you think this affects you as a leader?

Action — step into growth

Choose one area of life or leadership in which to practise a strong growth mindset. Create Unguarded Moments where you can explore your relationship to this area, and determine where you are seeing problems instead of opportunities. Commit to learning at least one new thing about this area or subject this week and create a plan to put your new knowledge into action.

CHAPTER 6

Connection: Creating Transformational Relationships

'The best effort of a fine person is felt after we leave their presence.' – Emerson

I once consulted for a company that lost $2 million in 12 months because its leader didn't value connection. The founder of this company, a man named Don, was a certifiable genius. He was detail-oriented, highly driven ... but not exactly a 'people person'. Now, social awkwardness doesn't disqualify anyone from becoming an Intentional Leader (as I can personally attest), but this guy had *zero* desire to build relationships with his leadership team, employees, or clients. To Don, his team, partners, and customers weren't people to collaborate with; they were chess pieces to be moved around the board of his vision.

Don wanted to be – and often was – the smartest person in the room. The best outcome of a meeting was when he did all the speaking. Don did not want conversations. He wanted agreement and compliance. To him, the perfect meeting was when everyone nodded their heads and accepted his marching orders without question; then, he could go back to hatching his plans for industry domination without interruption. Despite this, he wasn't a micromanager – in fact, just the opposite. He never held his team accountable because he couldn't imagine having those crucial conversations. When things didn't go well, he would flip his lid, but no one took his complaining, justifications, excuses, or even his anger seriously. After all, he wasn't going to fire them if they messed up. He was just one more obstacle they had to work around to get the job done.

The downward spiral started with a simple mistake. A prominent client needed to re-engineer and retrofit a large facility. Due to an internal error, the company's response only included half of the project's total cost. You'd think a mistake this grave would come to light quickly once things got rolling, but that wasn't the case. Instead, the project team worked diligently to complete the misquoted scope of work; as a result, the hole they dug kept getting bigger. During this time, neither the original mistake nor the subsequent challenges were communicated to the leadership team.

To make matters worse, the company needed to add more resources to complete the job. Instead of using their trained staff, they hired less skilled contractors. These contractors were undertrained and underprepared, and their many mistakes required expensive fixes. By this time, the client's trust had been eroded, so the company was forced to hire outside quality control inspectors to certify that their work was up to code. The cost overruns just kept adding up.

I don't know what was going through the heads of the project team, but I'm guessing it was something like, 'We have one more hurdle to get over, then everything will be fine. We'll make up the losses on the back end.' By the time things finally spun out of control, it was too late.

The worst part was that, because there was so little connection or accountability happening in this workplace, no one brought any of this to Don's attention. He didn't become fully aware of the problem until six months after the project started – at which point the client alerted him, 'We're laying the foundation for a lawsuit.'

By this time, Don's company had sunk over a million dollars into remediation, entirely without his knowledge. Ultimately, Don's company not only completed the project for half the price, but constant rework doubled their job costs. Between that and the lawsuit, they lost more than $2 million – all because no one in the company felt connected enough to Don, his goals, or the company's vision to speak up about a simple contract error.

In the end, the top players each took a small hit to their overall compensation. No one was fired. No one was disciplined. There were zero conversations about what had gone wrong and how they could avoid this in the future. It was all swept under the rug.

Hearing this story, all I could think was, 'This level of disconnection would never have played out this way under Intentional Leadership.'

Intentional Leadership is built on connection

The story you just read may seem extreme, but the dynamic I described between Don and his employees is more common than you might think. In fact, a recent Gallup poll of more than one million workers in the US found that the *number one reason employees quit their jobs* was a bad boss (or bosses). Another study by Career Addict found that 79 per cent of those surveyed considered poor leadership a factor in deciding to jump ship – and, of those, 40 per cent would consider coming back to the job if their boss were replaced.

Too often, employees and management seem to be playing on opposing teams. Each views the other as an obstacle to their objective – a necessary evil – rather than a piece of the same functional whole. Maybe you've even said it yourself: 'If only I didn't have to deal with *those* people, this job would be so much easier!' I understand. Not every person is easy to work with. However, I believe that *every person* – even the ones who seem to push everyone's buttons – has something to contribute to a thriving workplace.

Intentional Leaders understand that their real purpose is to serve and support their teams, no matter how challenging it can feel at times. The goal should not be to rule over an army of 'yes men', but to foster a collaborative culture that allows everyone to contribute. When we move into that space, we can invite our people to step up and do their best work, each day.

I want to be very clear: it is not our responsibility as leaders to change the people we're leading, or mould them into 'ideal employees'. It's not to demand their best and then expect them to deliver it with no further input from us. That might work for a few 'high achievers', but most people need more cultivation – and motivation – than that. They *deserve* more than that.

As we've learned throughout this book, our job as leaders is to 'tow the line', leading with our ideology and inspiring others to follow. And while Core Ideology is the trigger that helps people step on to our path, *connection* is what keeps them walking it alongside us.

If trust is the currency of Intentional Leadership, connection is the linchpin. More, it's the final death blow to Ghost Mode. It requires us to take all the inner work we've been doing throughout this book and put it into practice in real time with the people around us in a way we may never have considered before now.

Up until now, it's been all about *us*: our awareness, our Core Ideology, our ego balance. This is precisely how we've needed to work up to this point; we can't come out of Ghost Mode until we do the work to see where and how it's playing out through us. We need to understand our internal processes and get clear on our direction before we can pick up that line and start walking.

However, overcoming the final symptom of Ghost Mode, disconnection, requires something different from us than we've done so far. It requires us to hold the front of the line for our vision and ideology, while at the same time *prioritizing others' outcomes above our own*.

Intentional Leadership meets others' needs

All too often, we see leadership defending its own agenda. Don's company is a perfect example of this. The employees worked for one goal (making a pay cheque and covering their butts) and leadership was working towards something else (increasing revenues and outputs to grow the company). There were very clear strata within the organization, and a firm line of demarcation. There was Don – aka, leadership – and then there was everyone else.

That disconnection put everyone firmly in the realm of Ghost Mode. This made it hard for any real communication or collaboration to happen – even when the company's performance and integrity were at risk. The norm within company culture was 'everyone for him/herself'.

In so many companies for whom I've consulted, that line of demarcation – or rather, line of *disconnection* – between leadership and everyone else felt like an unbreachable barrier. I've worked with companies where leaders keep office doors shut 95 per cent of the time, even when they're not on calls or in meetings. I've worked with companies that had separate offices for executives across campus (or across town). These approaches make impossible the kind of unified culture and employee satisfaction glorified (but rarely explained) by popular leadership teachings. And so no matter how hard leadership tried, they couldn't get their employees on board with their vision for a better culture. Every initiative ended up dead in the water ... until leadership learned how to build genuine connections.

Here's the hard truth: leadership that serves only leadership's goals will *never* inspire loyalty. So what can we do instead? The answer lies in a simple but powerful psychology tool called Maslow's Hierarchy of Needs.

Every single person on the planet has basic needs for food, water, shelter, and sleep. When those are met, the primal stress of survival begins to lessen, and we can focus on attending to the next level of needs, which include safety and security. When those feel established, we can move on to social needs, and finally to our need for self-fulfilment and self-actualization through recognition, accomplishment, and purposeful living.

The *biggest mistake* that most leaders make is to assume that the people on their teams are fully meeting their own needs without guidance or direction. (Many of you reading this book will believe that your employees' most basic survival needs are being met at Levels 1 and 2: that they can eat, drink, and sleep regularly and without undue struggle, and feel relatively secure and safe in their daily lives. I want to acknowledge that this simply isn't true – especially for people in minimum-wage and entry-level positions, marginalized people or groups, people in abusive living situations, people struggling with addiction, and people unprepared for retirement or job change.)

Leaders can better meet their employees' Level 1 and 2 needs by providing fair and equitable wages, better benefits, and employee safety nets. They can create non-hostile, respectful, safe, and secure workplaces. They can create and enforce zero-tolerance policies regarding harassment, discrimination, and racist behaviour. (There's a lot to unpack here. In fact, I may write a separate book on this topic someday!)

Once the basics are in place, however, what does it take to create an atmosphere where true connection can happen?

Intentional leadership focuses not only on the bare minimum of Levels 1 and 2, but on the Level 3 social and belonging needs of their teams. When a leader shows interest in, and cares for, their employees, the team starts to build powerful connections: to the leader, to the organization, and to one another.

As the Pyramid shows, safety and security underpin social connection. When we have a sense of belonging, it supports our quest for self-fulfilment, which leads to advancement, which promotes self-actualization (i.e. being the best versions of ourselves). But if we as leaders don't set the bar for meeting needs around belonging, our people will never feel secure enough to reach for their highest potential in the arena of our collaborative work.

This isn't to say that people aren't capable of finding self-actualization outside of their work environment. It happens all the time. But those who do aren't invested in their organization as part of that process. In fact, if they don't feel that they're being supported at the social level, they will grow *away* from the organization as they advance up Maslow's Pyramid, rather than towards it.

In his book *Peak: How Great Companies Get Their Mojo from Maslow*, my friend and mentor Chip Conley takes this idea of identifying and meeting employees' needs and simplifies it.

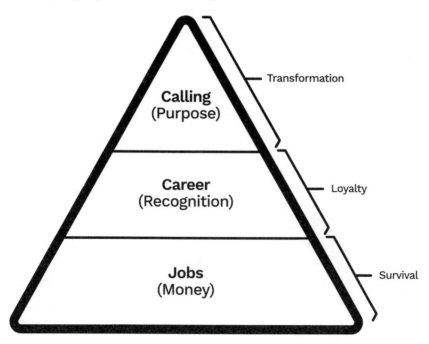

People who aren't receiving a sense of belonging at work (like Don's employees) are just there to do a job and collect a pay cheque. They're meeting their need for belonging in other ways – ways that have nothing to do with the organization, its vision, or its leadership. To them, work may feel like an obstacle to fulfilment, rather than a tool for it.

People invested in the organization at a social level are there to build careers, and to some extent will derive self-fulfilment and identity through their work. They're interested in producing outcomes for the organization because those outcomes create greater success in their individual careers. Many people in management roles fall into this category. They see their relationship with leadership as mutually beneficial.

But it's when we move *beyond* the self-focused goals of career and recognition and into purpose that things get interesting. Now, you have a situation where people are self-actualizing through their contribution to the organization. They will literally transform before your eyes. They will become the best, most empowered versions of themselves through – and because of – their work. They will go from having a job, to building a career, to chasing a calling. And the more this becomes apparent *to them*, the more committed to the work – and the Core Ideology behind it – they will become. It's an upward spiral.

As Intentional Leaders, our job is to pave that path to purpose through deliberate connection. And that starts by meeting others' need to *belong*.

The power of belonging

In his book, *Rock Bottom: From the Streets to Success,* Michael Cooley shares the story about how one moment with his CEO changed his entire career trajectory.

In 1990, ActionSystems was a 200-person customer relationship management software and consulting firm with offices in multiple countries. But when the savings and loan crisis happened, the organization nearly collapsed. In under a year, the organization had shrunk to just 14 employees.

At the time, Michael was working in one of the company's distribution warehouses. Honestly, he was shocked to still have a job; most of the other lower-tier employees had already been let go. But he was finally getting his feet under him after a stint in jail for gang activity, so he kept his head down and did whatever was asked of him.

The Friday before a holiday weekend, the CEO, a man named Robert Hall, gathered his few remaining employees in his office, and proceeded to lay out the situation and the reasons for the cost-cutting measures and layoffs that had taken place. It was all very data-based, very clear-cut. But then Robert directed everyone's attention to a flip chart behind him. On it were the names of the more than 180 people he'd been forced by the crisis to lay off. Tears came to his eyes as he read every single name aloud.

Up to this point, Michael had been hovering in the back of the room, half hidden behind a support column. He'd been through layoffs before. He knew the drill. It was only a matter of time before he was turned out, pink slip in hand, to join the unemployment line. But as he listened to Robert read those names, he leaned in. He moved out from behind the column. He felt his heart go out to Robert; he'd had no idea that the CEO cared that much about him and his fellow employees. There was an instant connection of empathy forged between them. When Robert met Michael's eyes across the room, Michael didn't bow his head; instead, he held Robert's gaze, and nodded his understanding.

From that day on, Michael committed himself to helping make ActionSystems a successful company again – not because doing so would allow him to keep earning a pay cheque, but because he wanted to work for a leader like Robert, who actually cared about his employees and considered them in his decisions.

Not long after that meeting, the company faced another serious financial shortage. The only way they'd be able to meet payroll that week was to ship $100,000 of product in under 24 hours. Because he now felt so invested in ActionSystems, Michael took on the task single-handedly. He worked more than 17 straight hours to get the shipment out on time.

Robert stopped by the warehouse to thank him personally. This additional layer of connection and mutual respect led to more conversations, and eventually to a formal mentor–mentee relationship and a deep friendship, which continues to this day.

Michael took on more and more responsibility as the company continued to pivot and adapt. By 1994, ActionSystems was on top again, and he accepted a promotion to production manager. By 1998, Michael stepped into a job as VP of a well-respected Dallas-based consulting firm, where he helped to negotiate a successful merger between ActionSystems and a Connecticut-based company that positioned both organizations to thrive in the digital age.

Without that single moment of connection, the trajectory of both Michael's life and career and the growth of ActionSystems would have been very different. Because Michael felt a deep sense of belonging – tapping into his social needs and laying the foundation for his self-fulfilment and growth – he made choices that moved both him and ActionSystems forwards.

Theodore Roosevelt once said: 'People don't care how much you know until they know how much you care.' Showing that you care about your team is the first step to building connection. But it can't be done lightly. You have to mean it.

Throughout this book, we've come to understand that all of us need to define and operate from a defined Core Ideology – and that if we want to create a high-performing organization, we must leverage Intentional Leaders who instil, support, and advocate for that ideology. Our values, purpose, and vision are our beacons, our guiding lights.

But after we come to a point where we can observe ourselves, embrace our unique Core Ideology, and manage our ego, we run into a question, and a powerful choice.

The question: 'Are we leading results, or people?'

For an Intentional Leader, the answer is *always* people. No pay cheque can buy the kind of loyalty that great leaders inspire. No bonus can inspire that level of commitment.

Some numbers-driven leaders may not resonate with this immediately. However, it's been proven over and over that real, sustainable results happen when people are engaged, valued, and working for a purpose. If you shift your workforce engagement from

33 per cent (which Gallup surveys indicate is the average level of engagement) to 50 per cent, what impact would that have on results?

Transactional versus transformational relationships

In leadership, we can build one of two kinds of relationships: transactional or transformational. These can be defined by the level of connection – or disconnection – happening between the players in any given moment, and at what level of the pyramid they are operating.

Transactional relationships are outgrowths of Ghost Mode. In the world of business, a 'transaction' is an exchange in which a product, service, or amount of money is offered in return for something else of value (such as money, time, or another product). In a transactional relationship, we don't have to be fully present to accomplish the task at hand. We don't have to support – or even acknowledge – the other person's needs. We don't need to build trust or communicate our Core Ideology. There is simply a quid pro quo exchange that asks, 'What do I need to give you in order to get what I want?'

In the case of Don's company, the relationship between leadership and employee was simple, singular, and purely transactional: 'I show up to work, and you pay me.' To be fair, Don treated his employees well in terms of salary, benefits, and other compensations, exceeding industry standards. However, employee loyalty only went as far as that pay period's direct deposit.

This is why, when things went south, no one thought, 'Wow, we've all been working towards this goal for a long time. It would suck if we messed it up. Maybe we should fix this.' No one cared or thought about how this giant error would impact Don and the company because his connection to his team was as shallow as a pay cheque.

In transformational relationships, people are working towards a shared goal, and they serve something more significant than the needs of the immediate group. Each person acknowledges the others for who they are and what they bring to the table. There's a sense that people are valued not just for the tasks they're handling right now, but for their ongoing contribution to the collective. Transformational relationships are part of a long game.

In our busy, technology-driven world, it's easy and tempting to retreat into our heads (or bury our heads in our phones) the moment things get tough. When we're stressed, overwhelmed, or overworked – as so many leaders tend to be – our default is often to disconnect from the people, demands, and activities that our role requires, rather than connect to them more deeply. We may also disconnect from our loved ones at home, our friends, and our outside interests because we simply don't have the energy to engage. Our ego dials up or dials down as we spend more time listening to the mental chatter and less time in our active space of inner authority. Trust falters. And unless we reignite our awareness and override that Ghost Mode switch, we can easily slip into that space of disconnection, dismissiveness, and transactional relationships.

I'll be honest with you: sometimes, the level of presence necessary to maintain our transformational relationships feels inconvenient. When there is too much coming at me or I'm under intense stress, all I want to do is close the door to my office and dig into the tangibles. But that's Ghost Mode. Instead, I recognize that those are the times when my door needs to stay open. If I disconnect, so will everyone I'm leading, and the intangible structure of our collaborative work will fall apart.

When I'm disconnected, I start to feel isolated, as if the weight of the world is on my shoulders: my mood, energy, and drive nosedives. Conversely, when I create connections, it feels like the burden of what we are trying to accomplish is spread out, so each individual needs to carry less. The feeling of overwhelm and suffocation lightens. The conversations I have, and the belief people have in what we are creating, recharges my batteries. I find the strength and excitement to carry on because I'm fighting a good fight, for much higher stakes than my compensation package. By showing up to meet the needs of those around me, my needs are met, and exceeded.

Does this requirement to connect sometimes feel like just one more thing on my already overflowing plate? Yes. Does it occasionally feel draining? Definitely. But the moment those thoughts start showing up, I know I need to connect *more*, not less. I need to show up with *more* presence, *more* inner authority, and *more* authenticity – because the cost of doing otherwise is too high.

How to create connection through transformational relationships

You may be asking at this point, 'Tim, *how* do I start building these connections?' Here's the answer: there are four simple steps to transform your relationships from transactional to transformational and cultivate a culture of belonging. They are:

1. Make a firm decision to lead people, not results.
2. Prioritize others' fulfilment above any other agenda.
3. Build and engage in every relationship as if you have no short-term goals.
4. Practise gratitude and appreciation.

At this point, you may feel confused. Why, when you've spent so much time focusing inwards to grow your self-awareness, strengthen your inner authority, outline your Core Ideology, and find a healthy zone of ego, are we suddenly turning the lens outwards?

The truth is, we aren't. To build the kinds of connections I have described in this chapter, you need to be crystal clear about how you're showing up and how you're supporting others' outcomes in *each and every moment*. It demands a level of self-awareness and self-regulation you may never have had to practise before. More, it requires transparency, authenticity, and vulnerability – all qualities that you can't fully access while you're stuck in Ghost Mode.

You see, if you want to be an Intentional Leader, connection and transformational relationship-building are not optional. But *how* you go about creating those connections will be unique to you. Your approach will be a direct reflection of who you are, what you value, and what vision you hold for yourself and your organization.

Results follow people

Several years ago, I popped into a local convenience store to grab a Diet Coke on my way into the office. The moment I walked in, I could feel that the atmosphere was very negative and depressing. The store was empty except for the cashier – a smallish woman with dark hair, glasses, and a frown that looked like it was permanently plastered to her face.

'Looks like she's having a bad day,' I thought. So, naturally, when I got to the checkout area with my items, I started a conversation with her.

'How's your day going?' I asked.

'Awful,' she replied, scanning my drink.

'Wow. That's too bad. But it'll get better.'

'I doubt it.'

'Maybe you should buy a lottery ticket,' I suggested.

'Why bother? I won't win.'

'Try it. You never know.'

I left the store feeling sad for this woman, who was so angry and depressed that she saw no hope for her day, let alone her life. I resolved to do what I could to cheer her up.

The next morning, I made a point to go into the same store at the same time. The atmosphere was still gloomy, but not as oppressive as the day before.

'How's your day?' I asked the cashier.

'Oh, you know.'

'Did you buy that lottery ticket yesterday?'

Her eyebrows rose, like she couldn't believe that I'd remembered. 'I did. Didn't win, though.'

For months, I saw this woman every day. We exchanged banter and greetings. Within a week or so, her attitude had shifted. When I asked her how her day was, she'd reply, 'At least it's not raining,' or, 'I get to see my daughter tonight, so that's good.' She hadn't become optimistic, exactly, but her attitude wasn't doom and gloom any more, either.

Two months later, she'd become more forward-leaning and engaged. Sometimes, she'd even initiate our conversations, telling me what lottery numbers she'd played the night before, or what she was watching on television. A few times, she even smiled at me.

And, for the first time in all these weeks, I started seeing other people in the store at the same time as me. I didn't think it was a coincidence. Through all this, we never learned each other's names. We were just two regular people having moments of connection.

Then, one Monday morning, I went into the store and she wasn't there. Instead, a young guy was standing behind the counter.

'Hey,' I said. 'Where's the lady who usually works mornings?'

'Short? Dark hair?' I nodded. 'She moved. Her husband got a job in Texas or something.'

'What was her name?' I asked. 'I never learned it.'

'Joy,' the young man said. 'Her name was Joy.'

Call me crazy, but I didn't find that the least bit ironic. I could only hope that, whatever Joy's next job was, she had a manager who cared enough to bring her out of her shell.

As leaders, we underestimate the impact of simply being who we are and doing what we do. When we lead from expectations, metrics, and results, we tell people that, 'These numbers and outcomes are our priority.' But if that's the case, it implies that the people creating the outcomes are *not* a priority.

I'd be willing to bet that Joy never felt like a priority to the manager of her workplace. She showed up as expected and did the bare minimum in her role (aka, scanning items and taking money). But she had no reason to bring her best self forwards, nor did she have a reason to care if people patronized her store and made the location successful. Her Level 1 and 2 needs may have been met (barely), but she was stuck in survival mode. She was just focused on doing the job – not on doing a *great* job.

As Richard Branson once said: 'Clients do not come first. Employees come first. If you take care of your employees, they will take care of the clients.' What Branson suggests is that when you invest in your employees by showing you care and fulfil their social and belonging needs as well as their basic survival needs, they will reward you by doing more than just the bare minimum.

Gallup's 2017 State of the American Workplace report revealed that only about 33 per cent of the workforce is actively engaged. The rest are either neutral (read: working for a pay cheque), or actively *dis*engaged and hating their jobs. That means that when clients, customers, and other employees interact with your people, they have a two in three chance of dealing with someone who just … doesn't care all that much.

And before you start thinking, 'that's just how people are', another Gallup report (2015) found that managers accounted for at least *70 per cent of the variation in engagement scores*. In fact, 79 per cent of employees said they wanted a better relationship with their manager(s).

If your people aren't engaged, you don't have a hiring problem, or a results problem, or even a 'management' problem. You have a *connection* problem. You're in Ghost Mode, and if you want to get out of it, you need to start putting people before results. Until you flip that switch in your mind, you will never be able to create your desired results.

Before you panic, I'm not asking you to stop caring about delivery, revenue, profits, or growth. Those keep your business thriving. But *engaged employees create those results naturally*. Jim Harter, a scientist at Gallup, explains: 'Engaged employees are more attentive and vigilant. They look out for the needs of their co-workers and the overall enterprise because they personally "own" the result of their work and that of the organization.' In fact, they'll go above and beyond to create them, because they feel just as invested in your company's success as you do.

As a CEO, I learned this early on. And so I made connection a regular part of my working week. Every other Friday (or whenever my travel schedule allowed), I would do what came to be known as my 'walkabout'. I would schedule about 90 minutes to walk the entire Atrion facility. I would say hello to every one of my 150-plus employees, drop in on group conversations, and get a feel for the mood and energy of each department. I'd also single out five to seven people for more extended discussions. There was no rhyme or reason, really; it was more like, 'I haven't talked to Ryan in a while. Let me see how he's doing.'

The one rule I had for these excursions was that I couldn't ask anyone to do anything for me. The focus was always on my team and what mattered to them. If we'd had a big win, I'd congratulate the department, and share how thrilled I was, but I never asked, 'Could you give me an update on that client?' Sometimes the conversation stayed in the realm of business, but more often, I found myself talking about kids, sports, hobbies, weekend plans, and even philosophy.

The more I got to know my team, the more they came to know me. The more my employees knew I cared, the more they cared – about me, and about Atrion. As a result, they worked their butts off to produce truly phenomenal outcomes without any whip-cracking, carrots, or sticks from me.

But here's the thing: I had to be authentic about it. I had to be consistent. Sometimes, the last thing I felt like doing was wandering around and talking about random stuff for an hour and a half. But I did it anyway ... and more often than not, I came back to my office feeling more energized, inspired, and purposeful, remembering not only what I was doing for them, but what they were doing for me.

Fulfilment is the best motivator

In addition to my walkabouts, I tried to spend 5–10 minutes every day with one individual, asking questions and coaching them towards the best possible solutions. I also started restructuring my meetings and conversations to allow my employees and managers to have more say in how things unfolded. In other words, I learned to let go of my need to have all the answers and instead invited my team to share in the creative process.

Fulfilment for those we lead isn't just a product of our connection with them – although that's the beginning. Employees are fulfilled when they have a sense of ownership – of co-creation. And when leadership spends all its time giving orders and trying to control outcomes, fulfilment goes down the tubes.

While my nature is to jump in and 'fix' everything once I've identified a problem (remember my story in Chapter 3 about Dave at Polaroid thinking I was a jackass?), I have learned to give equal weight to others' suggestions and input. This isn't because I don't know what needs to be done, but because I want everyone who works with me to have a sense of ownership, know that they're making a valuable contribution, and feel fulfilled by their work. This is another layer of the connection process, one built on trust and mutual respect.

At some point, I stopped giving directions to my leaders, and started asking, 'How would *you* handle this?' At first, this switch was challenging for my employees and me. My employees expected me to have all the answers. After all, I had conditioned them for years to think that I was the smartest person in the room. I was the consummate problem-solver, and I loved jumping in the middle of every fire drill. I had to learn restraint and patience. I will share that this lesson was one of my biggest obstacles to my leadership growth.

At first, when I asked my employee what they would do, they weren't prepared. Many struggled to offer suggestions. But with a little coaching or coaxing, they started to process the situation and provided their thoughts and solutions. If the idea was valid, I gave it the go ahead, even if it was different or less efficient than my way. If I didn't think the strategy would be successful, I'd coach the person through questions to a better solution. It wasn't about making them 'wrong', but expanding their point of view so they understood how the outcomes could evolve, and why. As I helped my team gain more perspective and insight, they started making better decisions. Soon, they were blowing my mind with their creative ideas. I found the strength of our collective was more potent than the power of any individual – me included.

The fact that my leadership team at Atrion was full of incredible people who cared about their work was no accident. They showed up that way because I learned when to guide them, when to coach them, and when to shut up and get out of their way.

What made this possible wasn't some supernatural flash of insight. It was the work I was doing around self-awareness. I had to get comfortable with not being the loudest voice in the room, and understand that valuing others' input didn't undermine my authority. I had to get my ego into a balanced place where I could make what my people were experiencing *more vital to me* than my personal feelings, goals, and ambitions.

Connecting in this way wasn't easy in the beginning. I was continually stopping myself mid-sentence – or, more often, apologizing after the fact when I realized I could have done better. It was humbling. But when I saw what was happening within my team, it got easier. Instead of being a commander, I became a guide. I was becoming a more effective leader, and consequently, my company became more successful.

Now, you may be thinking, 'That's great, Tim, but you were the CEO. It was your company. You had a stake in this whole "fulfilment" thing.'

Yes, I did. And so do you – even if it's not apparent yet.

For many years, I served on the boards of directors for several for-profit and non-profit organizations. The number one complaint the leaders of these organizations have is a lack of output from their middle management – the people who oversee the bulk of the company's operation, but haven't yet reached the tier where things like bonuses, profit sharing, and company shares become a factor.

If this is where you are, everything I've written still applies ... and then some. If you're currently looking to advance in your company, the fulfilment and engagement of the people you manage should be your *number one priority.*

Engaged people who know they matter – to you, to their peers, and to the execution of your team's projects – do better work. They go above and beyond. They don't clock out at 5.00p.m. on the nose and leave work unfinished. They don't do what Don's people did, and cover their butts to the point where it nearly capsizes the company.

For any leader to be employable, and to advance in position, they must create results – and unless you're a freelancer, or the only person in your department, you need a team to do that. People who deliver results get promoted. They get paid more. They earn more responsibilities. When we remember that *people* create the outcomes that move us towards our goals, it's easy to see why we should invest the effort to help everyone on our teams be as valued and fulfilled as possible.

Transformational relationships don't have an expiration date

I remember the day I asked one of our best clients to be a reference with a prospect. The client, Ben, was very loyal. Over 20 years, he referred nearly $40 million in business to us. Unsurprisingly, he always expected better than the best. When we delivered, Ben was over the moon. When we didn't … well, we knew it. He had a way of pushing us beyond our projected capacity; it was part of the reason I loved working with him. Our relationship grew over the years from a space of mutual trust and respect to a deep, abiding friendship.

On the day of our three-way call with my prospect, one of our techs made a colossal error that crashed Ben's whole network. Understandably, he was highly agitated and upset. Of course, I was panicking.

'Let's reschedule the call,' I said. 'It's more important that we get this taken care of.'

'Tim, just fix the problem,' Ben replied. 'I'll worry about the call.'

That day, Ben gave us one of the best references in our company's history, which in turn helped us to secure a $4 million contract. If I hadn't taken the time over the years to invest in Ben not only as a client, but as a person, this would never have been possible. We led with relationships, not sales results. We created ownership and co-creation with him and his organization. Because of our relationship, he was willing to overlook the fact that we'd just brought his whole network down. He trusted us to triage the problem and pull through.

My point is, you never know what will come about as a result of your relationships. You might discover that your warehouse manager is willing to work for 17 hours straight to help you meet a deadline, as Michael Cooley did for his CEO, Robert. You might find that your client is willing to go to bat for you, even when you've just made the biggest gaffe in history, as Ben did for us. You might find that your ex-employee is now a manager for your most significant prospect, and is willing to fast-track your proposal to her CEO because she's so excited about working with you again.

Nowhere in anyone's job description does it say, 'You have to care about your clients and employees.' But when we put in that extra effort to nurture our relationships, all the other stuff just seems to get easier.

When we brought on new clients at Atrion, we would bring them in to tour our facility. We'd walk them through the building, introducing them to the people who would be handling their projects. Almost always, they would step into my office and blurt out something like, 'The positive energy here is unbelievable!' And after a moment, it would sink in that all that energy would be directed towards serving them as our client.

That positivity, that extra effort … it was all discretionary. I didn't sit my employees down and tell them to 'be positive' or 'put on a good face for clients'. They did that because they were fulfilled in their work, invested in our success, and connected to our vision and purpose as a company. That was simply how they showed up every day.

Even though I sold Atrion several years ago, many of my relationships have carried forwards – whether through phone calls, LinkedIn or other connection methods. Many of my past employees regularly reach out to me for advice, perspective, or just to chat. In the same vein, I have hundreds of people in my database whom I can call any time I need a favour, a reference, or something else. This isn't because people 'owe' me something; it's because I've put in the energy to create a transformational relationship with them.

While your relationships may change as colleagues, clients, and employees move on to new roles and chapters in their lives, transformational connections are lasting. No matter how long it's been, you can reach out and pick up where you left off. They don't fade with time or distance.

The power of appreciation

It can sometimes seem unnecessary or overly sentimental to express our gratitude to the people around us for being part of our journey. However, appreciation is necessary in transformational relationships. It recognizes the work that has gone into the relationship, and lays the foundation for a new cycle of even greater cooperation and connection.

How to take your relationships from transactional to transformational

As leaders, we have a choice about how we show up and how we interact with others. We can choose Ghost Mode by being absent, distracted, unfocused, and disconnected. Or we can decide to be an Intentional Leader, creating connections and building relationships.

Unfortunately, we often spend too much time building transactional relationships. A transactional relationship focuses on what we can get from others. In this mode, we use people for their gifts, or talents, or what they can provide for us. Our needs come first and foremost, ahead of anyone else. We can stay in Ghost Mode while creating a transactional relationship by investing just enough to get what we desire. Don, whose story we shared at the beginning of this chapter, spent the vast majority of his time transacting.

Where transactional relationships are created out of need, transformational relationships are founded on what we desire to give to others. When we work on transformational connections, we concentrate on the big picture with the long game in mind. We intentionally focus on the connection, not the task at hand, or the result we are trying to achieve. The needs of our employees, co-workers, clients, friends, and family come first without any expectations. When building transformational relationships, we provide love, understanding, support, and inspiration. We cannot connect and create transformational relationships while in Ghost Mode. It requires intentionality and is open-ended, with no expectations.

When I teach about relationship building, I often say that transformational relationships are like pencils. If you take one pencil in your two hands, you can easily bend and break it. It doesn't take a lot of effort. But if you have five pencils together, they're a lot harder to snap. And if you have 10, or 20, or 100 pencils in your hands, they are pretty near unbreakable ... as long as they stick together.

Each time we make a real connection with someone, we add a pencil to the pile. Each time we help solve a problem, we add a pencil. Each time we have an authentic conversation without any hidden motives, or allow someone to take credit for their ideas, or prioritize that person's fulfilment and achievement above our own needs ... pencil, pencil, pencil. Each touchpoint strengthens the relationship, to the level where it can withstand an enormous amount of pressure without splintering.

Now, imagine if you had a ten-pencil minimum with each person on your team, or within your organization. How strong, cohesive, and unbreakable would you be, together?

This is what connection can do. And this is what disconnection – the final and most dangerous symptom of Ghost Mode – makes it impossible to achieve.

For my first decade as a CEO, I didn't understand this. I was a good manager and made 'leadership development' activities a priority when we had extra time and money – but they weren't mandatory. If you'd asked me point-blank, I don't think I would have said that people were Atrion's most valuable asset. Like most less-experienced leaders, it simply wasn't my philosophy.

My philosophical shift happened when I applied for a workforce development grant from the State of Rhode Island to train our team about new methodologies in our industry. Our request made it through the first phase of the process and the next step required a formal presentation to the Department of Labor and Training. I was determined to get this funding, because I knew this training would be a game-changer. So I started looking at how my competitors were framing their proposals, and what I could do differently.

It quickly became apparent that everyone else was focused on outcomes – what the grant would do for their company, their marketplace, the state economy. And so I started thinking, 'What would this training mean for the individual employee?'

I rewrote my whole presentation at the last minute. Following a simple idea from Steven Covey's book, *The 7 Habits of Highly Effective People*, I led with the end in mind. I asked questions like, 'How will this training change each employee's life?' The answers I got surprised me, and changed how I thought about investing in people and relationships. Then, I worked backwards from this end point to detail the results of the company, and the state.

I realized that, through providing this one form of training, I could help employees completely change their career trajectories. Their personal and professional development would drastically increase. Their expanded capabilities would allow them to earn more money – which they would then invest back into their families and communities, benefitting everyone they knew and cared about. In some small way, I began to realize that the more I invested in my employees and the more I cared deeply about them and their success, the deeper and richer our connections became.

Of course, there were benefits to Atrion as well. Because we would have more capable people, we could take on more contracts and make more money. That would allow us to hire more people and invest in *their* high-level training, which would in turn create even more income, opportunities, and jobs. With this model, our reach expanded exponentially.

That was the first time I understood just how crucial employee development was. From that day on, I put Atrion's money where its mouth was, and made training and development our highest priority. After 9/11 and the events I shared with you at the beginning of this book, we didn't always have the money to invest in those programmes; we did them anyway or found innovative ways to continue the development of our learning culture. The success of my employees – whether they stayed with Atrion for their entire career or not – benefitted everyone in their sphere of influence, including me.

Transformational relationships play a long game. They are about investing not just in a person's short-term contribution to the company, but in their long-term success and happiness. They are nurtured by a deep understanding and compassion for the individual, and a willingness to give and receive without attachment or expectation.

So how do you go about creating transformational relationships when you have short-term goals to meet and quotas to fulfil?

The answer is simple, and touches on all the things we've covered in this chapter: *understand what your people want – which is connection, fulfilment, and a sense of belonging to something greater than themselves – and help them get it.* That's all. Take your self-focused goals out of the picture for a while and see what happens.

* * *

Connection should always unfold authentically, in a way that works for you. But … if it feels *too* comfortable, you're probably doing it wrong.

Connecting deeply with your employees, clients, and colleagues is not something that comes naturally for most people. We aren't raised knowing how to do it; in fact, many of us (myself included) have past experiences that make true connection feel scary and uncomfortable. You will have to push yourself beyond your current comfort zone to start cultivating those transformational relationships. But when you begin to see them bear fruit, it will all feel worth it. I promise.

Harness the power of your Unguarded Moments. Reflect on times when you've felt genuine connection with others. Ask yourself, 'How do I want to connect with others, and how do they want to connect with me?' Then, take those actions as an Intentional Leader, even when they're not comfortable. Soon, you will start to see those pencils stacking up and you will be on your way to building unbreakable relationships.

Reflection

- Not every person is easy to work with. However, *every person* – even the ones who seem to push everyone's buttons – has something to contribute to a thriving workplace.
- If trust is the currency of Intentional Leadership, connection is the linchpin. It requires us to put all of our inner growth to work in real time with the people around us.
- Leadership that serves only leadership's goals will *never* inspire the loyalty of the people in the trenches.
- In leadership, we can build one of two kinds of relationships: transactional or transformational. Transactional relationships are a quid pro quo exchange that asks, 'What do I need to give you in order to get what I want?' In transformational relationships, people are working towards a shared goal; they serve something more significant than the needs of the immediate group.
- There are four simple steps to transform your relationships from transactional to transformational and cultivate a culture of belonging for your team:
    1. Make a firm decision to lead people, not results.
    2. Prioritize others' fulfilment above any other agenda.
    3. Build and engage in every relationship as if you have no short-term goals.
    4. Practise gratitude and appreciation.
- To be a more effective leader, take your self-focused goals out of the picture. Understand what your people want – which is connection, fulfilment, and a sense of belonging to something greater than themselves – and help them get it. That's all.

Unity of Thought and Action

Thought – is connection comfortable for you?

Take time to sit with what you've learned in this chapter. How do you feel about connection? What about connection comes naturally to you, and what feels challenging?

If some aspects of connection are uncomfortable to you, that's *great*. It means you are on a learning curve as a leader. Don't let the discomfort stop you from building new, more connected relationships; in fact, embrace it as evidence that you're shedding your *disconnection*!

Action – take baby steps to connection

- *Ask questions ... and listen to the answers.* As Dale Carnegie wrote in *How to Win Friends and Influence People,* the best leaders aren't interest*ing*, they're interest*ed*. Find a way to authentically want to learn and understand more about the people you're leading. Listen as you want others to listen to you. If you're not sure where to start, here are a few great (and safe) questions to start a conversation:
  - 'You could have worked anywhere. What made you decide to take a job here?'
  - 'What is the success you're most proud of?'
  - 'Where do you see yourself in five years?'
  - 'What's your favourite part of your job?'
- *Be authentic, consistent, and deliberate.* Take a few moments to plan out your conversations in advance to avoid those awkward pauses. However, be natural and conversational. Don't ask questions like you're reading from a checklist. *Commit to having at least three conversations a week during which you're not asking for anything.* In the Businessolver's 2020 State of Workplace Empathy, 78 per cent of employees responded that if their leader were more empathetic, they'd invest more discretionary time in their work. Create your own version of the walkabout so that you can have spontaneous connections and let people know you're interested in who they are, not just what they're producing.

- *Make yourself more accessible.* Leave your office door open unless you're on a call.
- *Create more opportunities for connection.* Even if you're busy, there are plenty of moments in your day where you can connect with someone on your team.
- *Say hello to everyone you pass on your way to your office.* Remember George and Anna from Chapter 2? That relationship might have been saved if George had been aware enough to just say 'Hi' on his way past her desk.
- *Take someone to lunch, or invite them to eat with you in the cafeteria or in your office.* According to the Bureau of Labor and Training's American Time Use Survey, 60 per cent of employees eat alone at their desks! As with the walkabout, don't ask them to do anything for you; just have a natural conversation.
- *Buy someone a coffee (or tea).* Talk about why they love their tall-double-shot-soy-vanilla-caramel latte so much, and share the story of that one trip to San Francisco when you had the best espresso of your life.
- *Turn to your mentors.* Ask them how they create connection in their own leadership roles, and whether they have advice or ideas from their own experience.
- *Remember that not all people want to connect at the same level.* You may notice that some people are more outwardly responsive to your overtures than others. Remember that this isn't a reflection on you. Not all people can easily verbalize what they're thinking. Just keep extending your hand, and they'll let you know how they want to engage.

Part III

CHAPTER 7

Leading from Within: Intentional Leadership in Action

'Revolutions go not backward.' – Emerson

In the autumn of 2014, I decided it was time to fulfil a commitment I'd made to my grandmother when I was eight, just before she passed away. My promise was to climb Mount Kilimanjaro.

I have an ongoing love affair with mountains, and Kilimanjaro is a unique climb for many reasons. One of the biggest is the climate. It's like a condensed trip from the equator to the North Pole. Where temperatures can reach more than 32ºC (90ºF) in the foothills, they can drop to -23ºC (-10ºF) or lower as you near the summit. Over 48km (30 miles) of the hike takes place at 3,050m (10,000ft) of elevation or higher. Almost 50 per cent of people who attempt the climb don't make it to the summit.

I knew this was going to be one of the biggest challenges of my life. But this trek was totally aligned with my Core Ideology of learning and exploration, and I knew the journey would test me in a way I'd never been tested before.

I booked the trek for October 2015, which gave me 12 months to train like mad. What kept me going wasn't the goals I set. It wasn't about completing 13km (8 miles) a day. It wasn't gaining a certain number of feet in elevation. No, what motivated me was the *vision* I was chasing. As I powered through those early morning runs, I kept that picture of Kilimanjaro in my head. I reminded myself of how much I would learn from this adventure and how I might pass on that knowledge to everyone else in my life. I thought of the commitment I'd made to my grandmother, and how much it would mean to her to know I'd succeeded. I thought of all the incredible lessons I'd be able to share when the climb was done.

That year, I logged more than 3,200km (2,000 miles) of walking, jogging, or running, plus over 240km (150 miles) of hiking and over 60,960m (200,000ft) of elevation gain. During test hikes at 1,830m (6,000ft) and above, I was able to maintain a relentless pace of 30 minutes per mile or less while keeping my heart rate below 120 bpm. Without my vision to propel me, I never would have been able to set those kinds of personal records.

When the day came to board my flight to Tanzania, I'd never felt more ready for anything in my life.

Boy, was I in for a wake-up call.

There were 16 of us in our hiking group, all experienced backpackers with significant high-altitude experience. We were excited about getting started. But the porters and guides who brought my group up the mountain set a much slower pace than I expected. They explained that the lack of oxygen at higher altitudes simply could not sustain a faster pace. In fact, pushing too hard could lead to acute cerebral and pulmonary oedema, and even death.

'Pole, pole,' they kept repeating, which I learned is a Swahili phrase that roughly translates to 'slowly, gently, softly'.

I didn't want to go slowly, gently, softly. I had trained for 12 months for this, and I was ready to go all-out! I could see that other members of our group felt the same. I kept reminding myself of Confucius's words: 'It does not matter how slow you go, as long as you do not stop.' But the fact was, I was growing more and more antsy.

On the second day, we started at the same grindingly slow pace, but as the day wore on, we faced torrential rain and sleet. Everyone just wanted to get to camp, so we increased our speed. 'Forget about *pole, pole*,' we said. 'Let's get out of this downpour!'

As a result of our overenthusiasm, we nearly killed half of our team. Two trekkers in our group ended their summit attempts and turned back. We should have learned our lesson then ... but we didn't. (After all, we were talking about a bunch of high achievers.)

On summit day (which actually started at midnight), we began at a slow, methodical pace, but as we got closer, we pushed harder. I was with the lead group, and our excitement was running high as the summit came into view. Despite warnings from our guides, we were moving too fast. A couple of guides and I did what should have been an eight-hour ascent in less than five hours. And I paid the price.

That day, at 5,640m (18,500ft) – less than 300m (1,000ft) in vertical distance from the summit and the realization of my lifelong dream – I got severe high-altitude sickness. For about 15 minutes, I battled a blinding headache, nausea, and a complete loss of energy. I had to stop several times to collect myself – but I couldn't sit still for too long, because the -7°C (20°F) temperatures coupled with 40km/h (25mph) sustained winds made it impossible to stay warm. At one point, I was violently ill by the side of the trail.

My intensive training and conditioning made it possible for me to recover and keep moving – but honestly, my biggest motivator was the thought that the guides would make me quit. After everything I'd done to get here, I wasn't going to let that happen.

I did summit Kilimanjaro that day, just as the sun was starting to rise. Above the thin red line on the horizon hung the moon, Jupiter, and Mars. It was breathtaking.

Reaching my goal was transformational for me. I literally conquered the mountain. In alignment with my vision and purpose for the trip, I also learned some essential lessons about myself and my work. They just weren't the lessons I thought I'd learn.

You see, I'd made the goal of summiting Kilimanjaro more important than the long-term vision (which in this case was coming back alive and healthy to share the fruits of my adventure). I put my vision in jeopardy because I couldn't see past the goal. And by pushing towards the goal past my endurance, I lost my connection to why I was climbing Kilimanjaro in the first place – which was to have a profound growth experience.

As a result, I share my Kilimanjaro story regularly with clients and workshop attendees. Not because I want to brag about summiting Kilimanjaro (although I won't lie, I'm pretty proud of myself), but because this story demonstrates exactly how Core Ideology supports us in setting and achieving leadership goals, and how dangerous it can be when we lose sight of our vision in pursuit of those goals.

Intentional leaders see goals differently

As leaders, goals are a big part of our daily lives. Yet, we struggle to complete our goals and objectives successfully. Research has shown that between 60 and 80 per cent of goals are never realized; they are abandoned before they are accomplished or set aside in favour of something new.

We all have goals and objectives we're seeking for ourselves, our teams, our organizations, and even for our communities and the planet. But when we lose touch with our Core Ideology in pursuit of our goals, or when we try to push too far too fast, failure is not far behind.

I live by a simple rule. As an Intentional Leader, I must never lose sight of my vision and purpose while pursuing my goals.

Unfortunately, I see this happen in leadership situations all the time. People are impatient. We want quick results so we can move on to the next thing. We want shortcuts. When climbing Kilimanjaro, I was so excited about making the summit that I stopped monitoring my heart rate, forgot to hydrate adequately, and pushed the pace too fast. The result was nearly disastrous.

In the business world, we aren't pushing ourselves physically, but the challenges are similar. The goals we set move our teams – and our entire organization – forwards. And rushing through crucial portions of our goals can sabotage our success just as surely as will pushing too hard on a mountain trail.

This self-sabotage happens often in business. We might close on an opportunity a day or two early and lose out on an even better deal. We might overestimate our team's capabilities and throw one too many unrealistic deadlines on their plates, killing morale and allowing other projects to slip through the cracks. Or, we might focus on acquiring the skills we need for rapid advancement within our organization without pausing to reflect on whether these skills and positions are aligned with our Core Ideology and life goals.

At other times, our issues with meeting our goals aren't due to moving too fast, but to moving without direction. We say we want to do things, and start strong, but we don't know how to stay the course in those moments when we're battling a downpour or throwing up on the side of the trail. Instead of finding the strength to persevere, we start making excuses, which leads to poor decisions, which leads to confusion within our team ... and the whole thing falls apart.

My new mentality is this: 'speed kills'. What matters is *velocity*, which is a combination of speed and direction. In other words, the issue isn't just in execution; it's in how we think about goals, and what those summits mean to us.

Your Core Ideology sets your direction. Your goals dictate your speed. When the two are aligned, you will always arrive in the right place at the right time – without killing yourself in the process.

Vision and goals are different

Many leaders confuse vision and goals, but the two are distinctly different.

Vision, as we learned in Chapter 4, is the audacious image of our ultimate destination and ideal. It's the inspiration for our progress, the pinnacle of our aspirations. It's not there to be conquered or surpassed, but rather to keep us pointed in the right direction and embolden us on our journey.

Goals are the mile markers on the road to our vision. They show us how far we've come, and how far we have yet to go. They keep us moving in the right direction. Goals are quantifiable and measurable. If our vision is the 'what', 'where', and 'why', our goals are the 'how'; they define the actions we take to move towards our vision. Establishing and achieving the right goals in your business and life will give you velocity in the direction of your vision, and increase your self-trust and self-confidence so you can stay the course through adversity.

John P. Kotter, a premier voice on how the best organizations create successful change, teaches about goals in a similar way. In his eight-step Change Model, goals are not set until the vision has been both created and communicated.

Goals are not the end game. They're not independent of vision. When we focus on goals alone, we're missing the point, and can no longer clearly see what constitutes 'winning the game' and what is simply … scoring a goal.

When leaders and organizations try to motivate people with goals, they inevitably fail. They create targets, metrics, and bonus plans to excite their teams, but this rarely works. Why? Because goals that aren't tied to a strong Core Ideology – values, purpose, and vision – feel hollow. They simply aren't enough to create the connection, inspiration, and sense of meaning that motivate people and teams to do the daily tasks necessary to create success. The thrill of reaching a goal won't sustain us on the days when all we want to do is hide in our office and close the door. It isn't a strong enough anchor to keep us from slipping into Ghost Mode.

Daniel Pink speaks about this in his TED talk, 'The Puzzle of Motivation'. His research (and that of hundreds of others) proves that extrinsic motivators don't work. As humans, we need more than a carrot and stick. We need to feel connected to something bigger than ourselves.

To see examples of vision and goals at play, we can look at two of the most famous men in America's history: Dr Martin Luther King, Jr, and President John F. Kennedy.

Dr King's vision was a world where everyone was treated equally based on personal merit rather than race or socio-economic condition. He expressed his vision in his famous 1963 'I Have a Dream' speech, which still resonates powerfully today.

Have we attained his vision? No. But it lives on even today, half a century after his assassination. We're continually moving towards that ideal and noticing where we need to work harder to achieve it. Many goals along that visionary path – including the passing of the Civil Rights Act, the legalization of gay marriage, legislation to create workplace equality, and the push for police and justice reform – have been met or are in process. There are many more to go.

In John F. Kennedy's 1962 'Moon Speech' at Rice Stadium, he stated: 'We choose to go to the moon in this decade and do the other things, not because they are easy, but because they are hard, because that goal will serve to organize and measure the best of our energies and skills...'

The task President Kennedy laid out – however challenging – was a goal. On 20 July 1969, the Apollo 11 mission landed Neil Armstrong and Buzz Aldrin on the moon. Mission accomplished. And because our goal had been accomplished, 1972's Apollo 17 was the final lunar programme.

During his speech, Kennedy even used the word 'goal'. And yet, so many leaders tout this as an example of vision. It's not. The goal was a moon landing. The *vision* was American supremacy in all areas – including the space race. Without that vision, the goal wouldn't have carried so much weight and meaning. It wouldn't have inspired a generation of physicists, astronauts, and engineers to devote their lives to its execution.

As Intentional Leaders, we must create and share our compelling Core Ideology before developing goals that support our aspirations. Our goals must then be tightly interwoven into the fabric of our vision so that all the actions we take in pursuit of those goals feel aligned with something more significant. Regardless of how many goals have been achieved, our vision will continue to act as a beacon, guiding the creation of new goals, and inspire our teams and organizations towards greater achievements.

The goal-setting process

Intentional Leaders don't just need to be self-aware. We need to become experts at identifying and setting goals for ourselves. Executing our goals proactively builds self-trust, reinforces our inner authority, and creates strong connections with those around us.

When the time comes for you to set goals – for yourself, for your team, and for your organization – you will always begin with your vision in mind, because your vision will inform every stage of this process.

When you come down to it, the goal-setting process is pretty simple, if you do things in the right order.

1. **Start with your vision.** What is the ultimate destination or ideal you're striving to create?
2. **Create your 'Big Goals'.** These are goals for your life, overall career, impact, legacy, and leadership. They're audacious, challenging, and focused on an outcome rather than specific actions.
3. **Commit fully to the Big Goal you've chosen.** Your Big Goal will take a considerable amount of time and commitment. Ask yourself: 'Am I actually committed enough to do this? Why do I want to do this now? How will attaining this goal further my vision?'
4. **Outline your Objectives.** Your Objectives are the smaller achievements or benchmarks that will combine to produce your Big Goal. They define singular outcomes, time frames, and measurements. They might be time-based (by month, quarter, or year) or metrics-based.
5. **Pick the Objective to address first.** Yes, you'll only be working on one Objective at a time. So do it right. Research the hell out of it.

6. **Set up your Action Steps.** These are the daily tactical actions you will need to take to accomplish your objective as outlined. Be extremely detailed with these. Set up time frames and systems for tracking your progress.

7. **Identify and prioritize Stand-alone Goals.** These are small things you want to do for their own sake: books you want to read, vacations you want to go on, creative projects you want to try. As with your other goals, pick one at a time so you don't get distracted or overwhelmed. *Note: I don't believe in Stand-alone Goals on an organizational level. Even things that seem like outliers (such as company holiday events, charitable donations, or office renovations) should be carefully considered and should reflect your company's Core Ideology.*

I'm not going to go into the particulars of goal identification and execution here. If you're unsure about how to choose or prioritize your goals, there are many helpful resources explicitly dedicated to this one skill. See the Recommended Reading section at the back of the book for more. However, seeing this process outlined for both personal and organizational goals may help you, so I'll share some examples in the next section.

One final note on goals: *never attempt to execute more than two at a time.* Research by Franklin Covey indicates that when leaders and organizations set one or two goals, there is a high likelihood that those goals will be achieved with excellence. When the number is increased to four–ten goals, it's likely that only one or two of them will be achieved with excellence. And when the number of goals in play is greater than ten, the likelihood of any of them being completed with excellence drops to zero.

Whatever the methods you use to identify and execute your goals, the process will always begin and end with your vision. Everything you do as an Intentional Leader should be a function of, and a step towards, the expression of a Core Ideology. If it isn't clear how your goals fit into your greater vision, they probably aren't helpful – or even necessary.

Setting goals for your Intentional Leadership

In Part II, we took an in-depth look at what it takes to overcome Ghost Mode and create Intentional Leadership from the inside out. Now, I will show you how to put these principles into play in your Big Goals, Objectives, and Action Steps.

But first, I want to address what you – and most aspiring leaders – are probably feeling right now. On the surface, the level of transformation and attention required from us to lead in this new way can be overwhelming – too big to be humanly possible. This is true ... *if* you try to do it all at once.

Intentional Leadership is a *journey*. Like the vision we created in Chapter 4 as part of your Core Ideology, it's an asymptote – an ideal we can constantly move towards but will never reach. As we learn, explore, and integrate, we move closer to our destination, but there will always be more to discover.

You don't have to master everything all at once. The important part is to commit to the climb, put your feet on the path, and '*pole, pole*'.

As Marian Wright Edelman, founder of the Children's Defense Fund, said of Dr Martin Luther King, Jr: 'He introduced me to the idea of taking one step, even if you can't see the whole stairway when you start.'

When I set my Big Goal to climb Mount Kilimanjaro, I had no idea what it would entail. I just knew that the time had come to do it. So I committed to the challenge, and then sat down to figure out what would be required to make this goal happen. During that process, I identified three clear Objectives: research, training, and the climb itself. These Objectives needed to be executed in that order if I wanted to be successful.

Before I started any physical training, I did a *lot* of research. Turns out, there are many ways to prepare your body for a strenuous, high-altitude climb. However, I didn't have three hours a day to do the weight training, high-altitude hikes, cardio, treadmill training, etc. that the experts recommended. Instead, I did my best to boil down the recommendations to something manageable. What would I have to do every day to develop the strength and stamina necessary to summit this mountain?

Early in my leadership journey, I learned that smaller action steps executed with a high degree of frequency were more effective than prolonged action less often. When I set daily repeatable action steps, I'm far more likely to reach my goal than if I establish weekly or monthly goals, which I will likely fail to execute.

Jim Collins talks about this in his book *Great by Choice* with the example of the 'Twenty-Mile March'. He postulates that if you trek from Maine to San Diego at a pace of 32km (20 miles) per day, every day, you will reach your destination faster than someone who varies their actions based on the weather, their desire, or other external factors.

When it came down to it, my training plan was simple: cover 8–13km (5–8 miles) per day, every day, regardless of the conditions. I also included several longer hikes at high altitude. These were the daily Action Steps necessary to execute my Objective, which was my preparation.

In theory, the plan sounded simple. In practice, it was *hard*. I trained in the baking sun, wild wind, and driving rain. Over the winter of 2015, I hiked my 8–13km (5–8 miles) a day in full winter gear while wearing a 13.6kg (30lb) weighted vest. Often, I was doing this at 4.00 a.m. before the start of my workday, slogging through blizzards or sleet or sub-zero New England temperatures.

Every time I completed a training day, I put a green checkmark on my wall calendar. When I didn't do it, I put a big black X. For me, visibility was a key component of success. I needed a simple scoreboard to determine if I was 'winning' or 'losing'. Every day, the results of my choices were hanging right in front of me. Once I got started, keeping the chain going became motivating in its own right.

When setting goals to become an Intentional Leader, ask yourself, 'What changes will be most helpful for me to make right now? What Objectives can I identify that will move me closer to the Big Goal?'

Many people confuse activity with progress. Working harder or doing more of the same thing doesn't always lead to the desired outcome. In some cases, this strategy will move you further from your objective. Instead of 'hustling', I recommend a thorough evaluation of the selected activity, including an evaluation of actions that are highly leveraged – meaning they will produce the greatest result with the least amount of effort.

Maybe your first Objective is to communicate your Core Ideology and values more clearly. Perhaps it's to become more connected with your team, or to observe and manage your ego so you can truly empower others. Once you understand your primary objective, you can use the information and exercises I've provided in Part II, along with your research, to create a daily action plan – the set of Action Steps necessary to execute your Objective. Remember, being busy doesn't mean you're moving forwards!

Be accountable for your execution plan for at least 90 days. Put your tasks on your calendar. Give yourself what you need to meet your daily goals. You will be amazed at how quickly the little everyday changes add up, and how much more connected you will feel to both your vision and your team as a result.

It won't be easy, especially when it comes to inner changes and self-awareness. There will be days when you just can't bring yourself to tackle the Action Steps you've chosen. There will be days when you just don't care about your commitment, and don't feel accountable. There will be times when you're exhausted from thinking so hard about your conversations, or from facing something you've been afraid of for a long time. This happens to everyone, and it's OK! At these times, remind yourself *why* being an Intentional Leader is aligned with your vision and Core Ideology. Your vision, along with some creative thinking, will give you the energy to push through, even when the goal itself doesn't.

To me, goals feel like mountains to climb. They demand preparation, training, and stamina. When you get to the top, you not only get the reward of the experience, but also a whole new perspective on yourself and the world – one you can bring to the next peak, and the one after that. But you need to have a *reason* to climb.

Climbing Kilimanjaro was a Big Goal – but it was perfectly aligned with my vision at that time in my life – which is why I knew I had to do it, and why I put in so much effort to succeed. Taking on something as big as Kilimanjaro was amazing, but it also took me 45 years to actualize. Depending on where you are in life, your Big Goals may not be summiting a mountain, writing a book, or starting a business. They may be to write your first blog, book your first public speaking engagement, or land a promotion. What makes a Big Goal significant isn't its 'wow' factor, but how it will transform you once you accomplish it.

If you still aren't clear enough on your vision to easily align your goals with it, go back and do that work now. Your vision doesn't have to be perfect; you'll revisit and refine it over time. But, as we've learned, goals without a vision to back them up are a waste of time – so don't set any, especially around Intentional Leadership, *until you have a working vision in place.*

Let me share another example of an Intentional Leadership goal.

I've dealt with dyslexia my whole life. At times, I was embarrassed and tried to hide the fact that I was struggling. I had to learn new ways to read, write, and speak. I was in my mid-40s, and I literally couldn't read something and say it aloud at the same time. I couldn't read a prepared message. I couldn't read a simple quote from a PowerPoint slide. Forget about reading from a teleprompter!

As a CEO and leadership facilitator, I spent a *lot* of time presenting. My inability to read what was on the screen in front of me was seriously getting in the way. Mostly, I'd just give up and try to go from memory – which only worked some of the time.

I knew I had to expand my public speaking and presentation ability. The need to communicate at a much higher level was integral to my leadership. So, I set a 13-week goal to improve my skill at reading aloud.

I created nearly 100 PowerPoint slides, each with a different portion of a famous speech. Every morning, I would spend 15 minutes reading aloud from those practice slides. I felt silly at first as I stumbled and stuttered my way through the words of Emerson, King, Roosevelt, and many others – but at least I was doing it alone and not in front of an audience. In time, it got easier. And after 13 weeks, I felt comfortable enough to try it in front of an audience.

Am I great at sight-reading now? Definitely not. But my discomfort with it is no longer something that gets in the way of my communication with my team, clients, and audiences.

This exercise had value far beyond just improving my presenting skills, however. As I did my daily practice, I realized that I rarely, if ever, shared with my employees and colleagues the fact that I have dyslexia. It was part of who I was – but I was also seriously averse to showing vulnerability. As a result, I tried to keep my dyslexia a secret.

I dedicated several Unguarded Moments to contemplate this line of inquiry. I began to see that I was often technical and sterile in the way I communicated. Focusing on facts and details, I limited how much of myself I shared with my audience. I wore a mask of strength, and never considered sharing any stories about my struggles. Clearly, this wasn't helping me establish the level of connection I knew I wanted.

Once my original 13-week goal had been met, I set another mid-sized goal: to open up more to the people around me. I started writing down stories about myself to share with people in our conversations. I wrote about the times when I had fully lived up to my core values of integrity, excellence, equality, freedom, and fairness – and when I had acted less virtuously than I desired. In very little time, I came up with nearly 200 short examples that I could share. I also wrote the origin stories of each of my core values, and how they've changed over time.

Now, I had a whole list of entry points to be more vulnerable with my team. But it also took some of the emotional charge out of my stories. Writing with the aim of sharing my core values, I saw events differently. I could share even my biggest mistakes without going back into the emotion of those moments. Ironically, creating separation and detachment from the story or struggle enabled me to create more durable and personal connections.

I made it a point to share at least one of these stories in my daily conversation. The results were nothing short of amazing. People opened up to me like never before. I started to get to know my employees and managers on a whole new level. We became genuinely human to one another, and create the transformational relationships I'd been striving for all along.

Realizing your goals as an Intentional Leader will force you to live outside your comfort zone. You don't have to do exactly what I did; these exercises were specific to my goal of becoming a better communicator. But when you are willing to get uncomfortable in pursuit of greater self-awareness, inner authority, empowerment of others, and deeper connection, positive changes will come much faster. More, you will increase your velocity, generate momentum and move into deeper alignment with your Core Ideology.

Most of all, be willing to change

When I was 22 years old, I decided I wanted to be a business owner. Not a technology freelancer (a position that was extremely popular in the information technology field). I wasn't interested in the solopreneur life or a small garage operation. What I wanted was to build something and be a legitimate leader in the marketplace, or what I called a 'true company'.

I didn't set a timeline or trajectory for this. I didn't even have a good idea of how I wanted to achieve it. But I did start asking myself questions such as, 'If I want to run a company, what's the next thing I have to learn?'

At the time, I was an individual contributor, writing code for a tech company alongside a team of six other people. My boss decided that our team needed someone to lead it, and started interviewing for the position.

I was present for this interview process, and by the time the third candidate walked out of the door, I knew I was more skilled than anyone we were interviewing. Not only did I understand the work, but I also knew the team, and I was committed to the company. In alignment with my vision, I felt this position could be the first step towards becoming a CEO. I'd been thinking about what I would do if I were hired to manage this team. So, I set up a meeting with Jim, my boss, and laid it all out for him: my technical abilities, my understanding of the market, my connection to the current team. I addressed what he must have been thinking: that I was only 22, that I'd never led a team, and that I would be the youngest manager in the company's history. Finally, I described what I would do in this management role, if given a chance, and shared my observations and ideas for things like team co-ordination and interpersonal connections.

The interview went well. A few days later, I was awarded the job. At home that night, I thought about what this new role would require. I looked young for my age. I had cubic zirconia stud earrings and new-wave hair (this was the 1980s, remember), and wore trendy clothes at a time when most IT professionals wore a standard blue suit, white-collared shirt, and red 'power tie'. As a developer, I had more leeway with my appearance, but I knew I was pushing the edge of what was acceptable. So, I decided I would professionalize my image, and dress for the position I wanted – that of a respected leader – versus the job I had. So, I removed my earrings, cut my hair, bought a suit, and added unique ties that allowed my personality to shine through.

I didn't resent the transformation – I embraced it. I wasn't focused on what I was giving up, but rather on what I was gaining. In the long run, becoming a CEO was more important to me than rocking my Flock of Seagulls haircut and acid-washed jeans.

What concerned me more were the other things I'd be giving up if I accepted this promotion. I loved writing code, and I was great at it. As a manager, I'd have to be OK with doing less programming and more direct interfacing with people and their issues. Was I OK with that, or would I resent the loss of my autonomy and creative freedom?

While in reflection, I realized that this was one of my Decisive Moments. This simple decision could put me on a path towards my desired future, or sidetrack those aspirations. I began to understand this was like the playground monkey bars. To reach the next rung, I had to release the hand behind me. To move forwards, I had to let go.

In the end, I decided that, like my hairstyle and clothes, writing code meant less to me than achieving my big goal. I chose to let go of what had defined me, and move forwards. And while my new position wasn't glamorous – in fact, it didn't even come with a new desk – it felt like a huge step towards my ultimate goal of business ownership.

I don't think enough people look at choices this way. They have goals for promotion, passions to earn more money, desires for more recognition … but they don't consider what they will have to do to realize those goals. This lack of awareness is an invitation to Ghost Mode, disconnection, and discontent.

If we want to achieve what we have committed to – for our organizations as well as ourselves personally – we also need to look at *what we are willing to sacrifice to get there.*

Double that if you want to be an Intentional Leader, and not just a boss.

When I'm setting leadership goals for myself, I don't ask myself what success looks like. Instead, I ask myself, 'What am I willing to sacrifice to achieve this?' Or, more brutally: 'What kind of pain will I accept?'

When you step into Intentional Leadership, you will be called to make sacrifices to meet your goals and follow the path of your vision. Probably it won't be your wacky style – thankfully, most industries are more accepting of individual expression today than they were a few decades ago – but you might be called upon to give up things like your aversion to 'small talk', your fear of public speaking or the excuses you make about your Ghost Mode habits and behaviours. When confronted with these, you will need to choose which you value more: your vision or your comfort zone.

People often ask me how I have accomplished some of my biggest goals – starting multiple businesses, creating an award-winning company culture, writing this book, etc. 'How did you stay motivated?' people ask me. 'I always wanted to do that, but...'

'What stopped you?' I ask them.

What follows is usually a litany of excuses – lack of money, bad timing, family, lack of knowledge, lack of resources, lack of confidence, and so on. But what really stops people from achieving their goals isn't the obstacles they encounter. It's their unwillingness to make the sacrifices necessary to overcome those obstacles. They want safety, security, and the guarantee that their efforts will be successful before they take a chance. They want the goal, but they don't want the pain.

Along your journey, you will have many opportunities to choose between the pain of creating what you want, and the pain of not having it. You will also discover that there are things you're not willing to sacrifice. Most of them will directly correlate to your core values, purpose, and vision. Remember my story from Chapter 4 about Ned, the florist, and how he got stiffed by my organization's CEO on the Christmas decorations? I wasn't willing to sacrifice my integrity to succeed in that organization. I might have accomplished some of my goals – but I would have moved *way* off track from my vision of who I want to become. Once I could see that, it was clear that I needed to pursue my goals elsewhere.

The lesson here? Before you set your goals, know what your non-negotiables are. Then, be willing to evaluate *everything else* when the time comes.

This is where Unguarded Moments come in handy. We need time and space to get a clear view of what's happening beneath the waves. Often, when we're fighting something we know we need to do, it's because we haven't done the deep dive into the underlying currents to find out what's going on inside us, and what we need to become aware of to keep moving towards our vision.

Much of the time, people resist the things they know they *must* do to become Intentional Leaders. Many times, the actions require strengths that they don't believe they have, or because the actions conflict with an idea they have about themselves.

The idea of growth versus fixed mindset applies as much or more to our beliefs about ourselves as it does to our ability to learn new systems and processes. Until we are willing to let go of our ideas about ourselves and what they mean about us as leaders, there is no room for new ideas to come in. We can't put new water in a glass that's already full.

For example, I once worked with a client named Brian, who hated public speaking. Whenever he had to present to a group of any size, he would become nauseated, sweat through his shirt, and even have full-blown panic attacks.

He had many reasons why he couldn't speak in public: introversion, anxiety, painful childhood experiences. But when he got promoted to a senior management position in finance, he knew he could no longer continue to function according to his previous paradigm. He simply could not be effective as a leader if he couldn't speak to his team.

We came up with a plan to gradually help him grow more comfortable with presenting. We broke down his goals like this:

- Big Goal: being an effective leader for his team;
- Objective: getting comfortable with presenting by:
  ○ researching strategies to increase competency;
  ○ creating a training plan;
  ○ scheduling his first presentation;
- Action Step: speak to small groups every single day so it becomes routine.

Because standing in front of a conference room was so nerve-racking for Brian, we decided to start small. Really small. For the first week of his training, he sat down with two people at a time in a small conference room. In week two, we increased this to three people, then to four. Eventually, his whole team was invited to these 'round-table' meetings, which he still led from his seat.

Once that started to feel more comfortable, we brought in a colleague whose speciality is working with public speakers on platform skills. He spent several hours with Brian, helping him understand powerful postures and how to overcome some of the physical challenges related to leading from the front of the room. From that point forwards, he conducted his meetings standing up.

Finally, Brian was ready to put his newfound skills to the test. He was scheduled to lead a presentation for 50 of his colleagues on a topic he was comfortable and familiar with. An hour beforehand, Brian started to sweat. But he didn't get sick. He didn't panic.

'I have the skills to do this,' he reminded himself.

And he did do it. Not flawlessly, but far more competently than he had ever imagined was possible. Now, Brian regularly leads presentations both within and outside of his company. It's still not entirely comfortable for him – in his own words, 'I'll never be a keynoter' – but it's a skill he can put to work in his pursuit of Intentional Leadership.

We all have ideas about what we are and aren't capable of accomplishing. Most of these are just that: ideas. Some skills may be harder for us to learn than others, and we may need help along the way, but nothing is out of our reach. The key is to make our vision bigger than our excuses, and lead with our strengths.

We are indeed hardwired to think and behave in specific ways. We have introverted or extroverted tendencies. We prefer collaboration over independent work, or vice versa. We prefer facts and details, or we prefer big-picture ideas. We're systems-oriented or holistic thinkers. Every human tendency has associated strengths and weaknesses. The key to overcoming our weaknesses is to lead with our strengths.

Brian was highly introverted and preferred to work independently. He was very strong in details, processes, and linear thinking. So when he decided to learn to speak in front of groups, we found a way for him to approach it that catered to his strengths rather than his limitations.

Don't allow your weaker areas to become an excuse for avoiding what you need to do as an Intentional Leader. If you find yourself saying, 'I can't do that because I'm [insert self-definition here]' consider creating some Unguarded Moments to explore this topic. Ask yourself how you can find a solution that highlights your strengths and still allows you to pursue your goals.

Creating velocity

Above all, Intentional Leadership is about becoming the best version of yourself, and leading from that place according to your strengths and Core Ideology. To do this, you must go where you are called, and do what others will not.

Goals for your organization can be planned and executed in accordance with the strategies that I've shared above. When you implement them, you will see a profound difference in your results. You can, and will, achieve breakthrough performance. However, remember this: your leadership journey begins where those concrete goals end.

True leadership mastery comes not from completing organizational goals, but from executing your personal goals in relation to Intentional Leadership. The habitual practices of creating space through Unguarded Moments, examining the deep currents of self-awareness, establishing inner authority, balancing your ego, and building meaningful connections call us into our best selves – not only as leaders, but as humans.

Unfortunately, we often view personal goals and development as extraneous – something to be done in our spare time. We see them as 'shoulds' rather than 'musts'. Right now, you may even be considering the work I introduced in Part II of this book as extracurricular, and therefore separate from the goal-setting work in this chapter. Nothing could be further from the truth.

It's the work we do within ourselves that allows us to create that all-important *velocity* in our leadership. The ability to convert 'shoulds' into 'musts' – to go over and above what is required and make the necessary sacrifices to reach our goal – is what sets apart Intentional Leaders from their managerial counterparts.

As a leader, I can choose the pain of staying stuck in the same place, reacting in the same ways, and creating the same results. Or I can choose the pain of becoming aware, changing lanes, challenging my ego, and letting go of my old self-definitions. If I'm not willing to sacrifice my comfort zone – my Ghost Mode – to achieve my goal, I need to find a new goal that is aligned with my Core Ideology and is big enough to motivate me.

Sometimes, the sacrifices we need to make to fulfil our goals for Intentional Leadership are clear. Other times, they're sneaky, and profound in ways we can't see from the surface of things. They are tied to the deep currents of our lives, and we need to dive far beneath the surface to see them. We must be prepared for that, too.

For George (from Chapter 2), saying 'Good morning' to Anna wasn't a must. It barely registered as a 'should'. But doing that one simple thing beyond what was required might have kept a valuable team member on his payroll. What would he have needed to sacrifice to do this? Perhaps nothing. Perhaps his internal definition of what it means to be a CEO. Only he can know.

'Must dos' are transactional. These are goals that create concrete results, and have clear pay-offs. The consequences (aka, pain) of not completing them are evident. We either pay our rent or forfeit our lease. We either meet our sales quota or lose our bonus.

However, our goals for Intentional Leadership are transformational. Their results may not be felt or seen for some time after we execute on them. But their cumulative impact will fundamentally change the way we lead and live.

* * *

Revolutions don't go in a straight line. But they always move forwards. So will it be with your Intentional Leadership journey. The road to mastery will lead you to unexpected places. Some will be exciting and interesting; others will be scary, frustrating, and uncomfortable. Embrace the adventure, and take the path that best suits your personal and professional development. You are doing the work, so trust that you are making progress, even if you can't see the results yet.

Reflection

- As leaders, goals are a big part of our daily lives. Yet, we struggle to complete our goals and objectives successfully. Research has shown that between 60 and 80 per cent of goals are never realized; they are abandoned before they are accomplished or set aside in favour of something new.
- *Velocity* is a combination of speed and direction. Your direction is set by your Core Ideology. Your speed is set by your goals. When the two are aligned, you will always arrive in the right place at the right time – and without killing yourself in the process.
- As Intentional Leaders, we must create and share our compelling Core Ideology before we can develop goals that support our aspirations.
- Executing our goals proactively builds self-trust, reinforces our inner authority, and creates strong connections with those around us.
- Along your journey, you will have many opportunities to choose between the pain of creating what you want, and the pain of not having it. You will also discover that there are things you're not willing to sacrifice. Most of them will directly correlate to your core values, purpose, and vision.
- Above all, Intentional Leadership is about becoming the best version of yourself, and leading from that place according to your strengths and your Core Ideology. To do this, you must be willing to go where you are led, and do what others will not.

Unity of Thought and Action

Thought – more activity does not mean more success

As an Intentional Leader, your growth does not happen by accident. It requires constant attention, hyper-focus, dedication, and commitment. The key to long-term success and progress is the creation and management of your personal development plan.

So, ask yourself: 'What is the most important goal that I should be working on to improve as an Intentional Leader?'

Action – you become what you do

Find the energy and commitment to create an Unguarded Moment. In that quiet space, brainstorm ten Big Goals that will lead to greater leadership mastery. Here are a few examples to get you started:

1. Create a culture of gratitude in the workplace.
2. Increase your presence with your team.
3. Create a short-term plan to build stronger and deeper relationships with your direct reports.
4. Find a key employee or stakeholder within the business and provide a deep level of mentorship.
5. Find a way to be more vulnerable and genuine with your team. Let them see the real you – warts and all.

Once you have your list of goals, implement the following process:

1. Remove any Big Goals from your master list that don't align with your personal Core Ideology.
2. Assess the remaining goals for leverage (the biggest impact with the least effort).
3. Prioritize your remaining goals from highest to lowest impact and importance.
4. Pick *one goal* from your curated list to get started.

5. Break down this one goal into Objectives and Action Steps.
6. Commit to executing the Action Steps for one Objective for a minimum of 13 weeks (90 days). Create a system to visually track your performance.
7. Commit to enjoying the growth!

CHAPTER 8

The Upward Spiral: Growing as an Intentional Leader

'Cause and effect are two sides of one fact.' – Emerson

Why, when someone corrects us, do we automatically fight to be 'right'?

One of my favourite tools to use with my leadership clients and workshop attendees is the 360-degree survey. Each person needs to answer 30 questions about themselves as honestly as possible. Each survey response can receive a score between one and ten. Once they've completed the self-assessment, each trainee needs to solicit ten colleagues, subordinates, or supervisors who will (anonymously) answer the same survey questions about them.

Low scores on any question reveal an area that needs work or attention – but ultimately, the scoring isn't what's important about this exercise. Far more revealing is the comparison between the participants' answers and those they received from their colleagues.

Before beginning a two-day intensive session with ten leaders at a well-known firm, I asked the attendees to participate in a 360-degree survey. As we reviewed the results as a group on day one, we could see where the attendees' and their observers' perceptions were perfectly aligned. Similarly, we could see a clear misalignment between the observer and the self-assessment. In other words, we could see where people were intentional, and where Ghost Mode was at play.

One woman was struggling with her leadership assessment. She was stuck on the fact that several of her feedback partners had rated her very low in key areas. As she had ranked herself very high in these areas, she felt that she deserved much higher scores. She couldn't stop obsessing over it.

'Let's not focus on the score,' I suggested. 'Why don't you review this tonight and find one or two areas where you feel you can make improvements to close the gap.'

However, when she went home that night, this woman didn't do that assessment. Instead, she went back through her results and simply removed the disagreeable parts. Consequently, her average results shifted to a place that aligned with her perspective.

Honestly, I was shocked. She'd missed the whole point. She'd completely erased someone else's observation of her because it clashed with how she perceived herself. Rather than asking, 'Is this observation helpful? Is there something here I can learn?' she just ... deleted it.

If, as you read this story, you found yourself thinking, 'I would never do that. How could anyone be so ... un-self-aware?' I challenge you to look at your own life more closely. Chances are, without thinking very hard at all, you can come up with a time (or three) when you acted irrationally because you felt challenged.

I've experienced many cringe-worthy moments in my time as a leader, business owner, husband, father, and human. When I think about them now, I know I could have reacted differently, said something more helpful, or just kept my mouth shut. There were times when I didn't know what came over me, or how I got myself into that situation in the first place. But in those moments, I still did what I did. The benefit of hindsight is that we can learn from these moments instead of relegating them to the 'shame' bin and pretending they never happened.

Nothing slaps us back into Ghost Mode quicker than the feeling of being challenged. But no matter what you're up against, one thing is certain: you can't hang out in Ghost Mode and grow as a leader at the same time. You absolutely must be willing to be present, engaged, and open, even when – especially when – your first reaction is to want to delete, delete, delete.

Overcoming ourselves and our reactions *in real time* is the final frontier of Intentional Leadership. None of us was born with the skills to respond perfectly in all situations. Life is an imperfect teacher, and as a result, we learn imperfect reactions and coping skills. Overcoming this conditioning takes practice, commitment – and most of all, self-awareness. It's what all the work you've done so far in this book has been preparing you for.

To be clear: the goal isn't to become so 'Zen' that nothing triggers us. It's to recognize our patterns and work on them so we can respond appropriately, instead of react irrationally. This requires converting our 'shoulds' to 'musts', and doing what others won't do – in this case, stop wishing you'd done something differently, and actually start *being different*.

Once we get more comfortable managing our responses, we can actively seek out challenges and embrace them as opportunities for growth.

Getting in the ring

Once we become aware of our inner dynamics, we need to keep working with what we learn until self-awareness becomes our natural state. Only then can we begin the *real* work of Intentional Leadership, which happens in real time across various situations.

The best way I can explain this is to share the story of how I found my martial arts teacher in Denver, Colorado.

Several months after my sensei's wife kicked my butt and gave me the wake-up call that changed my life, I graduated from high school. Like many kids from rural areas, I joined the military. I chose the Air Force because I was already into technology and it seemed like the most exciting path. For the last three-and-a-half years of my Air Force career, I was stationed in Denver, Colorado. Now that I wasn't travelling so much (and wasn't being pummelled by the physical training), I wanted to get back into martial arts. I dropped in for a couple of classes, one at a Karate studio and another at a Judo school. I didn't like the instructors or their methods, so I didn't go back.

I decided that if I was going to invest time and energy into finding the right teacher, I might as well be efficient about it. I started calling various schools and speaking to the owners and head instructors. I ended up calling about 30 different schools across many disciplines, and asked each teacher the same set of questions, including: 'How long will it take me to earn my black belt?' Most teachers responded with some variation of: 'It depends how hard you work, but probably seven months to two years.'

Then, I got on the phone with David, the man who would eventually become my teacher. His reply was different from what I'd experienced with the others.

'Let me answer your question with a question,' he said. 'Why is it so important to you to get your black belt?'

Taken aback, I said, 'I'm not sure. I guess because it will mean I've mastered the art.'

'The way I look at it,' David replied, 'the black belt isn't a culmination of your journey. It's the starting point. You learn all the basic stuff you need to know on the way to your black belt, but it's only after you cross that line that you become a *true* student of martial arts.' He continued, 'If all you are looking for is to get your black belt fast, then we are probably not the school, and I am not the teacher for you.'

Coming out of Ghost Mode – being more self-reflective, creating your Core Ideology, managing your ego and learning to create real connection – is like earning your black belt. The Four Pillars of Intentional Leadership you learned in Part II of this book are like the *katas*, the routines you practise until they become automatic. By the time you earn your black belt, those motions are ingrained deep in your bones and muscles. You don't have to think before you execute them. They are part of who you are.

Once the Four Pillars of Intentional Leadership have become part of your everyday reality, you will be ready to become a true student of the art. You will be prepared to take what you've learned and put your skills to work in real time.

When you're sparring in martial arts, it's not just about you and your moves. It's also about your sparring partner. You need to be aware of their actions, their emotional state, their strengths, and their weaknesses. You need to adjust your moves and reactions in response to theirs.

Fighting in the ring may not be the most politically correct analogy for leadership, but it's apt nonetheless. When you get into real-life situations as a leader, it's not just about you anymore. You're constantly responding to the people across from you – and those people are each having their own experience of you and the situation. Sometimes, you must adjust how you're showing up so you can bring out the best in a person and create that dance-like flow that happens between evenly matched sparring partners. Sometimes, you need to pause and let everyone breathe and regroup. Sometimes, you get blindsided, and have to pick yourself up off the floor. And sometimes, you have to pull your punches, so you don't cause real damage.

Bruce Lee said: 'When one has reached maturity in the art, one will have a formless form. It is like ice dissolving in water. When one has no form, one can be all forms; when one has no style, he can fit in with any style.'

Maturity in the art of leadership isn't about enforcing your vision, will, or personality on to anyone. It's not about how strong or fast or smart you are. It's not about being the star of the show. It's about adjusting your technique to bring out the best in everyone and accomplish your shared goals.

The best leaders know how to be like water – adaptable. They have the awareness to know what each situation, conflict, or challenge requires according to the shared vision and goal, and shift accordingly.

To do that – to be the water – we first must learn the moves. Self-awareness, our Core Ideology, managing our ego, and practising connection should be automatic functions. But from the very beginning, long before we get to black belt level, we need to get in the ring and practise these skills with others.

In the case of Intentional Leadership, this means doing three key things on an ongoing basis. I call these the Intentional Leadership Mastery Practices. They are:

1. Ask for, receive, and integrate feedback.
2. Consistently seek opportunities to improve.
3. Become a teacher as well as a student.

When we make these things part of our daily lives as leaders, we begin that black belt journey into mastery.

The first is by far the most important. Therefore, we will spend significant time on it in this chapter. If you master only that practice, you will create trust, connection, and empowerment in a way that 98 per cent of leaders will never manage.

The second practice is an extension of the first; we can learn a lot about where to improve and what risks to take through the feedback we receive.

The final practice is different, but incredibly rewarding. Leadership isn't just about the leader. Teaching what you have learned allows you to develop the next generation of Intentional Leaders and create a living legacy.

Fight, flight, and feedback

As a leader, you should continually seek feedback. Whatever that feedback looks like – whether it comes through formal surveys, casual conversations, or unsolicited comments – you should treat it as something to be embraced. It is never something to fear or avoid, even when – *especially* when – it pushes your buttons.

Why? Because feedback shows you where you are 'being the water', and where you are being the giant rock obstructing the middle of the stream.

When you first get in the ring as an Intentional Leader, it's like being a newbie in martial arts. You'll feel like you're floundering. You'll need to make big, coarse, sometimes ugly adjustments until you get the feel of what's happening. Over time, it will be less about the significant shifts and more about refinement – but you must get the mechanics down first. Over time, you'll get better, and your impact will increase.

The thing is, if you get in the ring, you must be willing to get hit. Getting harsh feedback *does* feel like getting hit, especially at first. In fact, it's sometimes harder than taking a physical punch. Few things in the world make us want to run, hide, hit something, point fingers or burst into tears more than receiving feedback we don't want to believe or aren't ready to hear.

We all instinctively want to deflect, rationalize, minimize, or simply ignore information that doesn't chime with our ideas and ideals about ourselves. (Remember our discussion about cognitive dissonance in Chapter 3?) When 'negative' feedback comes our way, the first thing we want to do is justify, blame, make others wrong, or beat ourselves up. We instantly revert to Ghost Mode as our fight-flight-freeze response is triggered.

Before we move forwards, I want you to know that this is normal. We are emotional beings. When under stress, we see everything through a lens of fight, flight, or freeze. We categorize people, situations, or stimuli as 'friends' or 'foes'. It's an instinctual response left over from a time when threats were more physical and literal, and death was a common by-product of failure. However, this 'caveperson' response causes us to react to *any* perceived threat as we would to a sabretooth tiger or a charging bison. Our reptilian brain hijacks our more-evolved self.

When you feel 'attacked' by someone's feedback, it's as if you actually *are* being attacked. Your physiological response is the same as if you were confronted by a charging bison or a leaping tiger. This reaction has been studied for decades, and is referred to as an 'amygdala hijack'.

In his 1996 book, *Emotional Intelligence: Why It Can Matter More Than IQ*, Daniel Goleman defines an amygdala hijack as a personal, emotional response that is immediate, overwhelming, and out of measure with the actual stimulus. He concludes that certain incidents trigger a feeling of emotional threat that affects the body as significantly as a physical threat would.

Here's how it works. The brain captures stimuli from the world through our five senses. The output of the sense organs is routed to the thalamus. The thalamus sends part of the stimuli to the amygdala (the emotional part of the brain) and the rest to the neocortex (the logical, thinking part of the brain).

The amygdala is evaluating the stimuli looking for a friend or foe match. When a match is found, the fight, flight, or freeze reaction is triggered and the rational portion of the brain is hijacked. All of a sudden, we are running off pure emotion and instinct. While this is an advantage when being chased by a sabretooth tiger, it is hugely detrimental in the boardroom.

During an amygdala hijack, blood is diverted from your vital organs to your limbs to prepare you to run or fight. You might feel your ears, cheeks, or neck getting red-hot. Your amygdala prompts the release of stress hormones like cortisol and adrenaline, which heighten your perception of the threat while preparing the body to act.

This response leads you to identify the current situation as extremely urgent, dangerous and demanding of immediate attention. In some respect, you're asking, 'Do I eat it? Or does it eat me?' For a short time, you're literally out of control, because the neocortex processes information about 40,000 times slower than the amygdala. This creates a gap of several milliseconds between our emotional reaction and logical response.

A lot happens during this gap. Our bodies are flooded with hormones to enable our next reactions. Oxygen is diverted from our brains and vital organs to our limbs, to give us extra fighting (or fleeing) power. When an amygdala hijack occurs, it almost always leads to irrational and destructive reactions.

The key to breaking this cycle is to create space between your perception of the threat and your response to it. If your parents or teachers ever told you to 'take a deep breath and count to ten' when you were pissed off, they had it right; it takes your body 5–10 seconds to recover from a hijack condition. For this reason, creating a pause is the simplest and best way to give your rational brain time to catch up. You'll often see great leaders create this space in interviews; they'll repeat the question they were just asked, or take a deep breath before they start to speak. They're not just being thoughtful. They're stopping the hijacking process in real time.

You need 5–10 seconds (or longer) for your rational brain to catch up with your instincts. Until that happens, you're in full-on Ghost Mode. You've been hijacked by your lizard brain, and almost any decision or response you make in this state will be the wrong one.

It's during those moments when we've been mentally and emotionally hijacked that we make most of our mistakes as leaders. We say and do things we regret later. We dismiss people when we should be listening. We make assumptions about other people's motives, and act on them as if they were true.

In the modern, sabretooth tiger-free world, hijacking is not only unhelpful, it's also contagious. If a colleague's feedback causes me to become hijacked, my irrational response might incite that person's own irrational response. Drama and chaos inevitably follow.

A friend of mine, Arjun, is the CEO of a mid-sized company. During a meeting, one senior employee made a comment that Arjun interpreted as being out of line. Needless to say, the discussion got ugly. As they locked horns, everyone in the room became uncomfortable. When the meeting ended, Arjun stormed back to his office and typed an email to the employee, the gist of which was basically, 'get on board or get out'. The employee was blindsided, and a storm erupted among the entire management team. Several came close to tendering their resignations.

Clearly, Arjun was emotionally hijacked before his senior employee had even finished his thoughts. As a result, Arjun interpreted the comment out of context. The employee was, in fact, on board and invested. He had been suggesting improvements, not dismissing the entire project.

Several hours later, Arjun told me what had happened – and boy, was he still hijacked.

I asked, 'Why did you send that email?'

'I wanted him to know I was unhappy. I know I could have done this differently. But I do this all the time; I just overreact.'

Arjun had no idea that he was being hijacked by his own stress response. After the fact, instead of admitting that he was at fault, he tried to justify that his reaction was acceptable and warranted. Later, he acknowledged that it had all been a misunderstanding, and that he could have done things differently – but he still couldn't grasp that the pivotal moment wasn't when he clicked 'send' on that email. The moment when things went wrong were the seconds between his employee's comment and his decision to act on his emotional response.

When we decide how to act or react during that crucial time when our brains are hijacked, *we will likely follow through with our decision* even after our physical stress response calms down and new information becomes available. This is tied closely to the mechanism of cognitive dissonance we learned about in Chapter 3; our brains will justify our initial beliefs even in the face of overwhelming evidence. Arjun was stuck in this cycle not because he wasn't smart and rational, but because he hadn't trained himself to recognize the moments when he *wasn't* rational.

Feedback supports emotional intelligence

Emotional intelligence is an essential skill for anyone who wants to be an Intentional Leader. *Psychology Today* defines emotional intelligence as 'the ability to identify and manage one's own emotions, as well as the emotions of others'. In many ways, you've been practising this throughout our work together in this book. To manage your responses skilfully, you need to know who you are, what you value, and why you feel the way you do. You need to have a healthy ego so you can be honest and clear about what's happening in your inner world.

But self-management is only half of emotional intelligence. The other half is understanding how to work with the emotions and responses of others to help them feel empowered, valued, and connected. You can't understand how to work with others' feelings and responses if you don't know what they are. Feedback not only reveals how you are showing up to others, but also who *they* are and what they value.

We all see the world through a unique lens. This lens is created by our values, our personality, our strengths, and our experiences. The first step towards creating emotional intelligence is realizing that not everyone perceives people, situations, or the world in the same way. I had an experience at Atrion that really brought this home for me.

Heather was a middle manager on our team who had worked with me for many years. We had a great working relationship and a high level of mutual respect. One day, Heather came into my office and told me that she needed time off for an elective surgery. She shared with me that she was getting a breast reduction, which she hoped would drastically improve her quality of life.

I listened as she explained that this was nothing major, that she would only need a couple of weeks off and that she expected no complications. Basically, what I heard was that this surgery was no big deal; she just wanted me to know what was going on. Of course, I approved her request for time off without a second thought.

A month later, Heather had her surgery. Just as she anticipated, she was back at work a few weeks later, and seemed to be back to her old self. I figured she would have told me if there was anything else I needed to know, so I didn't mention it in our conversations. (Also, I didn't want to overstep our professional boundaries by asking personal questions about her sensitive procedure.)

About three months later, Heather came into my office and asked, 'Can I give you some feedback, Tim?'

'Sure,' I said, curious. 'What's up?'

'I'm really disappointed in you right now. I had this surgery and you never once asked how I was doing. I came back and it was like nothing ever happened. It feels like you don't care about me the way I thought you did.'

I felt like I'd just been gut-punched. I could feel my mind being hijacked by my stress reaction. I took a deep breath, rubbed my suddenly sweaty palms on my pant legs, and counted to five in my head before I spoke.

'I'm so sorry. I thought it was a sensitive subject, and I wasn't sure you'd want to share more information with me. But you're right, I should have asked. Do you want to tell me about it now?'

Heather shared more about the procedure, her recovery, and how both had affected her entire life over the last three months. In the end, she accepted my apology, and we left the conversation feeling like our relationship was back on stable ground.

Inside, though, I felt shaken. How could I have been so insensitive?

From our first conversation, I had concluded that Heather's surgery was minimal – like having a tooth pulled or something. I understood now that she had downplayed the extent of it, probably because she didn't want to seem weak or like she was attention-seeking. But not only did I know nothing about what breast reduction entailed, I'd also transposed *my* feelings about the surgery on to my expectations from her.

For a variety of reasons, this surgery had been the top priority in Heather's life for nearly half a year. Once finished, it would reshape her body and self-image for the rest of her adult life. She'd needed to prepare for it, go through the painful process of it, and recover from it. Once she'd started to heal, she looked different. People saw her differently. It was a *big* deal.

The reason that the conversation hit me so hard wasn't my failure to follow up with Heather, although I did feel like a jerk for that. It was the realization that, for the last three months, I'd been *expecting her to feel like I felt*.

Where else had I been doing that in my life? Where else had I expected people to see things as I saw them? Where else had this dynamic been playing out in my work, my family, and my friendships? And, now that my eyes had been opened, what was I going to do about it?

This skill of 'putting myself in someone else's shoes' is one aspect of emotional intelligence I still struggle with. I tend to rank things in my head in order of importance. If I'm not worried about something, I can be offhand about it – but I understand that to someone else, this issue might be life-threatening. By putting Heather's surgery in the 'no big deal' bucket in my head, I had created a situation where she felt I didn't care about her well-being – which was the furthest thing from the truth.

If I want to keep such a misunderstanding from happening again, I need to ask what's happening with someone, and how they feel about it. The more I continue to develop the ability to understand my own thoughts, feelings, and emotions, the more I can truly appreciate and understand someone else's – but I must also recognize when there is a gap in our shared understanding.

Heather's unsolicited feedback opened my eyes to the reality that I still needed to become a better leader. I needed to be more intentional, more empathic, and more compassionate. As leaders, we all have blind spots where our perceptions differ from those of our team, colleagues, and clients. However, once we identify them, we can give them more focus and attention, and eventually minimize (if not entirely erase) them.

Is it any surprise that, as Dr Travis Bradberry claims in *Business Insider*, 90 per cent of top performers in the workplace have high emotional intelligence? And that, even though they have high emotional intelligence, these top performers continually seek feedback, self-assess their decisions, and monitor their social interactions.

Operating with emotional intelligence takes practice. Most of us aren't naturally aware of how we show up in a social setting. However, with time and commitment, we can learn to know ourselves and others better.

Tools such as personality assessments, surveys, and feedback forms are great ways to learn where other people are coming from, and help you adjust your communication style to their needs. However, all of that still leaves us with a certain amount of guesswork. The only thing that can fill that gap is honest, raw feedback.

Therefore the best thing we can do as Intentional Leaders is to create strong connections – because in the end, the best way to know how someone is feeling is to invite them to tell you.

How to ask for, receive, and integrate feedback

The best way to get actionable feedback is to ask for it. You can do this through formal channels, such as the 360-degree survey I use with my leadership trainees. You can do it in one-on-one conversations, or in groups. Whatever method you choose, it's crucial to maintain an open channel for your employees and team members to share their thoughts and feelings about you, the company, and one another.

Here are some general rules for asking for and receiving feedback.

1. *All feedback is valuable*, regardless of how it is delivered or what language is used.

2. *All feedback contains golden nuggets.* As Intentional Leaders, we must sift through our conversations to find these valuable insights.

3. *When asking for feedback, be pointed and specific.* Don't ask generalized questions such as, 'What did you think of the presentation?' Instead, ask, 'Today, I tried something different and shared a personal story during the presentation. How could I have made the story more relatable?'

4. *Echo what you think you've heard.* For example, you might say, 'Shauna, thank you for the feedback. This has given me some fresh insight and several actionable items. Do you mind if I share what I believe I heard? First, I heard that you think I did a solid job of delivering a difficult message. You also felt that I should have addressed some of

the participants' concerns before jumping into the proposed solution and asked for their input. You liked how I ended the presentation on a positive note. Did I miss or misconstrue anything?'

5. *Ask 'Is there anything else?'* After you've echoed what you think you've heard, ask the person if they have anything additional to add.

6. *Always say 'Thank you'.* This seems so simple, but it can make a world of difference to everyone, especially when it comes to difficult feedback.

Be willing to learn

In November 1994, my business partner, Charlie, and I ran into some severe business challenges. Atrion was just seven years old and growing rapidly. At that time, I managed the technical operations and back office while Charlie handled sales and marketing.

Charlie was a born entrepreneur and full of amazing ideas. We would joke that he never sold the same solution twice. I was a technical geek who focused on creating processes and systems to provide the best possible long-term solution for our clients. Over and over, Charlie would come up with ideas that solved our clients' problems, but which we had never delivered before, let alone streamlined or systemized. And since I managed technical operations, I was in the position of doing all the clean-up when these untested solutions went sideways. We always made it work for the client, but at what cost?

This all came to a head when my partner sold a brand-new client a brand-new technology solution that I'd never seen or touched. The IT equipment was shipped directly to the client – which meant that my team and I had to unpackage the product, perform the quality check, configure the solution for the client's environment and cut over the solution without ever having laid eyes on it. Back then, the Internet was in its infancy. There was no way to go online and watch video tutorials, download a product operational manual, or even see a visual of the product. Instead, we had to figure it out on the fly while the new client stood over our shoulders, trying to learn about his new solution from the 'experts'.

In the end, we finished the project and got things up and running for the client, but I'd had enough. Charlie and I sat down and I laid out all my frustrations. There was a lot of anger and resentment built up on both sides. We both were hijacked and the conversation escalated into a shouting match. We sounded like 11-year-old kids in the playground. And then, Charlie said something that changed our lives – and Atrion itself – forever.

'Tim, if you think my job is so effing easy, why don't you just do it?'

I don't remember exactly how the argument wrapped up. I just kept hearing Charlie's question in my head. On my drive home, I wondered, 'What *would* happen if we swapped roles?' Charlie was a more-than-competent engineer; he'd have no problem fulfilling the technical side of my job. And while I didn't know a lot about sales, I was confident that I could learn.

The next day, I approached Charlie with the idea of swapping roles. To my surprise, he wholeheartedly agreed. We decided to make the switch in July, at the start of our fiscal year.

I spent the next seven months learning everything I could about sales. I read more than 50 books, attended seminars and trainings, achieved the Dale Carnegie Sales Advantage certification and even became an assistant facilitator for the Sales Advantage programme. I was primed to tackle this new role.

In mid-June, we got a decent-sized opportunity to work with a new client. 'Do you want to take this one?' Charlie asked.

'Absolutely!' I replied.

The competitive side of me wanted to blow this out of the water. I worked with the prospect using all my newfound knowledge, created a unique solution design, built the proposal, and submitted our bid.

We made it to the final round and were invited to present our solution to the prospect's review committee. I did a presentation for the client that (in my opinion) was pretty kick-ass. Then, we waited, and we waited.

Finally, we got the phone call. I closed the door to my office, sat down and took a deep breath. 'Hello?'

'Hey, Tim,' said our client liaison, Darrell, 'I wanted to let you know that we loved your proposal. You did an outstanding job on your presentation…' Darrell went on for another two or three minutes about all the great things we'd accomplished during this sales process. I was feeling confident and thought that Darrell was going to award me the contract.

Then he said those fateful words: 'However, we've decided to stay with our incumbent.'

I sat there, stunned. Honestly, I wanted to cry. I said to myself, *Tim, act like you've lost before.* Taking a deep breath, I tried to keep my voice steady as I thanked Darrell for the opportunity. I expressed my pleasure in working with him and his team.

I don't know what possessed me then, but in a moment of clarity and vulnerability, I said, 'Darrell, I don't know if you know this, but this is the first solo sales contract I've handled. I learned a tremendous amount during this process and I absolutely loved working with your team. I hope that someday we can work together.'

I continued. 'I have one favour to ask. Can I take you to lunch to talk about what I could have done differently to earn your business?'

Darrell and I went to lunch the following week. His feedback was some of the most helpful I've ever received.

'You did everything right,' he told me. 'Your numbers were right on, and I loved the plan you created. But you had no idea where we were in our relationship with our incumbent. We don't hate our current vendor. We don't love them, either – but in the end, it came down to "the devil you know". If you had asked, you could have positioned your solution differently and won our trust.'

I sat back in my chair. 'Wow. I'm so glad I asked.'

That one conversation informed my approach to sales for the next ten years. And after every deal, whether I won or lost, I always offered to take the client to lunch and get their feedback. If we lost the deal, I would ask questions like, 'What could I have done better? What would have helped me to win your trust?' If I won, I'd ask, 'What made you choose Atrion over the other bidders? What exactly did we do to win your business?'

Sometimes, the feedback I got from these conversations was challenging. I was told more than once that I was arrogant or difficult, and that the client didn't like my 'I'm always right' attitude. I accepted this. I *could* be arrogant and difficult, particularly when it came to the technical stuff, because the truth was I was *really* good at what I did. I used to justify my behaviour because I always had the clients' best interest in mind. However, as with the situation with Dave in Chapter 3, letting my ego get the better of me almost always created a less-than-fantastic outcome. So, I adapted my reply to less-than-positive feedback to some version of, 'Thank you for the feedback. I understand how I could have come across that way, and I apologize. I'll do better next time.' And I made sure I did do better the next time.

Other times, the feedback was terrific. I once worked with a woman who was new to her position. While she was an experienced manager, she had never worked in tech before. She asked a lot of questions that to seasoned technologists seemed rudimentary, even silly. Mindful of my ego after some of the other feedback I'd received, I told myself to be patient. She later told me that she loved working with me because I made her feel comfortable enough that she could ask me anything. She knew I didn't think less of her because she was still learning. This feedback felt good to receive and showed me that I was making progress on the 'arrogant and difficult' tendencies. And, because it showed me what my client valued in our relationship, it was just as valuable as the negative feedback for shaping how I dealt with clients in the future.

By the time I stopped handling sales for Atrion, my close rate was 88 per cent, in an industry where the average is 33 per cent. It wasn't because we were always the cheapest, or even the best on a technical level. It was because I was willing to manage my ego, learn to apply emotional intelligence and think like the client.

The second Intentional Leadership Mastery Practice I shared earlier in this chapter is 'continually seek opportunities to improve'. All feedback, no matter how it's delivered, contains a kernel of truth. It's our job to figure out what that is, and act on it.

Too many people expect feedback to be perfectly worded, delivered at the right time and full of instructions for how to become better. When it doesn't show up that way, they dismiss it as rude, mean, off-the-mark, or entirely invalid. This is wrong.

It's tempting to judge the timing and content of feedback. However, this is just another excuse for us to discount or disregard it. Remember, all feedback contains golden nuggets of information to fuel your growth as an Intentional Leader. Instead of writing it off because of how it's delivered, take the time to understand it. Search for the kernel of truth that exists within.

And above all, remember: the person giving you feedback is not responsible for teaching you how to integrate it.

Grow where you're hijacked

In addition to feedback, we can continually improve by always having one area of our life or work where we're focused on growth and learning. I talked a bit about this in Chapter 7, but I want to expand on it here in the context of feedback and emotional intelligence.

When looking for areas to improve, it's helpful to look at the places where we are most easily hijacked. Working in these places isn't comfortable, but it will create noticeable results in a small amount of time.

People get hijacked when they feel threatened, when they receive feedback, or in moments of confrontation. Less-than-ideal performance at work, too much stress, or personal struggles can also contribute to amygdala hijacking. But this internal co-opting can also occur in benign daily leadership situations that, for others, don't present an issue. One common example of this is public speaking.

Speaking isn't just about presenting information; it's about connecting with your audience. The best speakers put their skill of emotional intelligence to work to bring people along with them. And while some people are natural orators and performers, most of us have a steep learning curve if we want to be effective on stage.

I've shared my difficulties with public speaking due to my dyslexia. But even once I had become comfortable reading from slides, I would still get hijacked when I had to speak. Many people experience this. Before going on stage, they go into deep stress. Sometimes they sweat, or pace, or have trouble breathing. Some people become physically ill, and experience diarrhoea or vomiting. By the time they get on stage, they're not thinking clearly, and this affects their performance. After all, when you're dealing with hijacking, you can't present the best and most relatable version of yourself.

When you're in that hijacked state, you might do small things to reassure yourself until you find your flow. In my early days of public speaking, I would always stick one hand in my pocket. If there was loose change in there, I would jingle it. I did this subconsciously. I never realized I was doing it; it was like a self-soothing mechanism. There are videos of me presenting to large groups where you can barely hear my voice over the rattling of my pocket change.

As I learned to be more self-aware in the moment, I was able to stop doing this. Before going on stage, I would take everything out of my pockets. Doing that became a soothing ritual in itself. It was a small shift that made a drastic difference in my efficacy.

My client, the CEO of a consulting firm, asked me to assist with a substantial investment. Their company had selected three vendors to present their solutions to senior leadership and the board of directors. I participated in all three vendor presentations.

Ten minutes into the last presentation, the lead salesperson had only gone through two slides. My client leaned in and raised a hand. 'Excuse me for a second.' When the presenter had stuttered to a halt, he said, 'Can we hurry this up?'

I expected some sort of a pivot from the presenter – maybe a question like, 'What's most important to *you* to learn about this opportunity?' Instead, the presenter started to sweat. He nodded nervously … and launched right back into his prepared material. Only this time, he spoke twice as fast. I could barely keep up with him. Unsurprisingly, that sales team didn't get the contract.

In any leadership moment – whether we're on a stage, in a meeting room, or across the desk from one of our team members – we need to read the situation and let our observations provide feedback. Are we jingling the change in our pockets? Are we rushing to get through our key points or talking over people's heads? Is our audience falling asleep? In those awkward moments, we're like those people at a party who keep telling their stories even though no one is listening. We don't need to do more of what we're doing. We need to change our approach.

So much of the time, we experience stress because we don't know how to self-monitor. It's hard to change course in the moment and 'be the water' if you can't use feedback to gauge where you are, or if you're being hijacked in the situation. When we put the Four Pillars of Intentional Leadership to work in real time, we become self-aware enough to realize not only how we're feeling, but also how others are feeling. This is the beginning of real emotional intelligence.

If the leader of that team had been equipped to read my client's body language and responses, he might have changed the tone or even the content of the presentation and gone on to win the contract. Instead, he allowed himself and the whole meeting to be hijacked by my client's frustrated comment (which, granted, could have been delivered differently, but that's another conversation).

Chances are, you're already exercising emotional intelligence skills in some areas of your leadership. That's why my advice is to 'grow where you're hijacked'. The areas where you're already doing a great job are not the ones that need your immediate attention. You'll see the most significant shifts from placing your attention on the things that trigger you.

Doing this work requires a firm grip on your inner authority and a healthy ego balance. Without it, you will easily slide into unhelpful patterns such as people pleasing, indecision, and judgemental thinking.

Being emotionally intelligent doesn't mean burying your feelings, thoughts, or observations. It merely means meeting people where they're at. When you are confident enough in your Core Ideology, inner authority, and strengths, it won't feel like a hijacking when you're asked to change your approach.

It's easy to reach a place where you can coast in your leadership. But the status quo never leads to greatness. If you want to get to the next level, you'll need to apply what you've learned in new and different ways. It's that 'black belt' refinement. Where can you speak better, communicate more clearly, be more approachable? Where can you help people feel even more connected? Where can you be more inspiring? These are all questions that will feel exciting once you've reached a high level of self-awareness and inner authority.

Becoming an Intentional Teacher

When I reflect on my career, the thing I'm proudest of isn't how big Atrion grew, or how much money we made, or even how many awards we won. It's how many leaders we created.

Our employees used to say that we weren't an IT company; we were a leadership factory. Dozens of our people went on to become CEOs, CFOs, CIOs, and senior managers at other companies. Our people were the truest measure of our success. It was amazing to watch their progression from novices with little-to-no experience in any leadership role, to practitioners of Intentional Leadership with a high degree of mastery. They started as white belts and became black belts. They gained what some refer to as 'unconscious competence'.

You've probably seen the 'conscious competence' model, which looks like this:

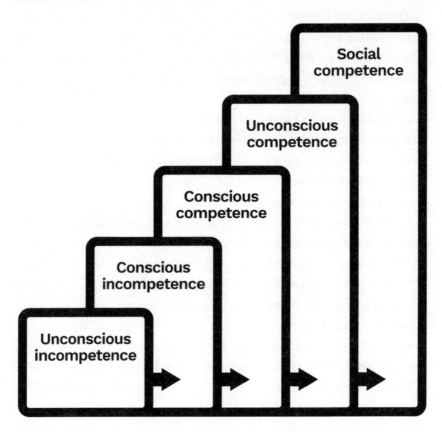

This model was initially introduced in 1969 by management trainer Martin M. Broadwell, who described it as 'the four levels of teaching'. This model defines a four-stage process of progressing from incompetence to competence (or mastery) in a new skill.

An individual is initially unaware of how little they know or don't know. They are unconscious of their incompetence. Many leaders start their journeys at this stage.

As individuals gain knowledge and experience, they begin to realize what they don't yet know and understand. They recognize their incompetence as they consciously continue to acquire the skills that will lead them to competence. This stage is 'conscious incompetence'.

As their competence increases, leaders apply their knowledge, skills, and experience with a new level of effort and thought. They recognize problem areas and potential blind spots. Still, intense concentration is required to perform, because their skills are not yet automatic. This is 'conscious competence'.

Eventually, a leader's ability is deployed without constant monitoring or examination. At this level, new skills can be actualized effortlessly. Tasks and critical decisions are made without conscious effort. As a result, leaders are confident in their ability to adapt and create success. Leaders at this fourth and final stage have acquired 'unconscious competence'.

Our aim as leaders is to become unconsciously competent in the Four Pillars of Intentional Leadership – to make self-awareness, inner authority, ego management, and connection such a part of us that they become as natural as breathing. When we reach this level of mastery, we have earned our leadership black belt, and our journey into Intentional Leadership truly begins.

When we reach this stage, we realize that the conscious competence model is two-dimensional. Intentional Leaders add a third dimension – a Z axis – to this model. That extra dimension is *shared competence*. This is where Intentional Leaders become coaches, mentors, and teachers. They consciously develop the next generation of leaders by sharing knowledge, explaining their processes, and creating opportunities for application. Most importantly, they demonstrate the 'why' for achieving greater leadership mastery.

Why invest time and energy into shared competence or teaching? Because the best way to learn something is to teach it to someone else. 'While we teach, we learn,' said the Roman philosopher Seneca. Teaching exercises a different part of your brain. As you prepare to teach, you review your material through the lens of experience. You seek out key points, organize the information in a coherent structure, and find ways to simplify the complex.

Exploring these new dimensions of your subject matter will teach you things you could never learn from study and experience alone. More, teaching helps you retain the information you are sharing. (In fact, Edgar Dale, creator of the Learning Pyramid, proposed that we retain 10 per cent of what we hear, 20 per cent of what we read, 50 per cent of what we discuss, 75 per cent of what we do, and 90 per cent of what we teach!) Teaching will help you become more intimate with the knowledge, experiences, and wisdom you have been developing; in many ways, it makes you an even more advanced student of the practice.

During my leadership programmes, I often recommend that attendees find one area of interest from the day's material and share the information with someone in their sphere. The students who do this exercise almost always return the next day with more insightful and probing questions. Their depth of understanding and their ability to contribute drastically increases from one single episode of teaching.

Some leaders rebel at the idea of becoming teachers. There is power in knowledge: the more you accumulate, the more relevant and indispensable you become. However, this is just another expression of Ghost Mode. No one was ever made less by giving to someone else.

There are many ways to teach. Not all of them involve standing in front of a classroom or mentoring a protégé. In fact, I would argue that Intentional Leaders teach without even realizing it. Our every word and action is watched by our teams, colleagues, and clients. We are role models, whether we like it or not – and when we bring our 'A' game, we become the people others want to emulate.

From this place of leading by example, more structured teaching or mentorship isn't a big leap. When you put some thought into it, you will find the method that works best for you. When you do, I promise you will learn more about leadership than you could have ever imagined, and this expansion will inspire you to keep learning.

Your Intentional Leadership black belt training

The more self-aware you are, the easier it will be to refine your approach and exercise your emotional intelligence, both in pursuit of your goals and in daily leadership situations. Even when you feel like you've reached a place of mastery with regards to the Four Pillars of Intentional Leadership, don't stop devoting attention to them.

More, don't wait to get in the ring and start learning to manage your responses and accept feedback in challenging situations. Intentional Leadership is not a theoretical practice; it's an experiential one. You can't just think about it. You must live it.

There is no point at which you will become self-aware enough to make this easy, so don't put off implementing what you've learned in this chapter. No matter how much inner work you do, you will still need to make daily corrections. You will stumble. You will get hijacked. You will make mistakes. It's OK. It happens to everyone. Now that you're aware of the issue, you can practise handling it in a way that is to your advantage.

If you're not sure where to begin, make a list of the types of situations and conversations where you routinely get hijacked. Do conversations where your authority is challenged really push your buttons? Do situations where you must accommodate others' fears and foibles make you want to scream?

As you do this, you're going to want to justify your actions and reactions – as Arjun did with his angry email. Resist that temptation. Instead, try to be objective about your reactions and what outcomes they created. At what point did things go south? What could you have done better?

Once you've identified an area of growth, make it a priority. Practise having conversations and receiving feedback in new ways. Communicate with your people what you're trying to improve. Ask for feedback about what you could do better, and how they felt in those challenging moments. And, when possible, sincerely apologize for those times in the past when your behaviour was less than admirable.

Once you've begun to learn to manage your responses and receive feedback in a positive way, you can turn your attention to the other half of the emotional intelligence equation: managing others' responses.

Everyone experiences the 'fight-flight-freeze' reaction. When they don't understand that they're being hijacked, people usually react in one of four predictable ways: get aggressive and go into 'fight mode'; ignore, deflect, or run away from the challenging situation (flight); shut down, disconnect, and stop communicating (freeze); or go into what psychologists call 'accommodation', adapting their behaviour to please or appease others (flight).

As a leader, you need to learn to recognize when someone is being hijacked, identify how they are reacting, and respond in a way that meets their needs.

In my early days as a leader, I was much more comfortable with the 'fighters'. I knew how to diffuse conflict. But when it came to the fleers and the freezers, I had less confidence. I had to override my natural tendency to be directive and prescriptive, and forge a connection through inquiry instead. I found that if I could draw someone out with conversation and questions, they would come out of their stress response and begin to communicate productively.

This took a lot of practice for me. It felt more 'emotional' than what I was comfortable with or accustomed to. The first time an employee cried in a meeting with me, I froze like a deer in headlights. I had no idea what to do. Should I take this person's hand? Pat their back? Hand them a tissue? It was only once I got over my discomfort and started listening that I figured out that this person didn't want comfort from me at all. They simply wanted someone who could listen and understand. They wanted someone to understand and care for what they were going through.

It took me a while, but I finally figured out that my discomfort with other's reactions wasn't a sign that they were doing something wrong.

It was a sign of my emotional immaturity in work relationships. As a leader, it wasn't my employees' job to be what I needed. It was my job to understand what *they* needed and support them so they could do their best work.

Never stop growing

Even when you think you've got something down to a science, you should always stay open to feedback. I remember presenting at a leadership conference to a diverse audience of men and women from all over the country. I walked offstage feeling confident that I'd just delivered one of the most powerful presentations of my career. However, the second person to approach me didn't agree.

'In your whole presentation,' she observed, 'there were no stories about women or people of colour.'

My immediate thought was, 'I talked about Martin Luther King. I talked about Gandhi. Don't they count?' But as I took a deep breath and counted to ten, I realized that she was right. The famous leaders I quoted may have been diverse, but the everyday leadership stories I shared were not. I had plenty of stories that featured women and people of colour, but I hadn't included any in this presentation.

'Thank you for your insight,' I said, shaking her hand. 'I'm so glad you said something; I will do better next time.'

We can always do better. When we put on our leadership black belts, every day is an opportunity for refinement.

* * *

Intentional Leadership is truly a lifelong journey. It's a path, a practice, and an art. Over time, you will make it your own. You will transition from disciple to master. You will continue to grow and develop by teaching others. You will impact more people than you will ever know, and influence others more than you will ever realize.

Most of all, you will be a force for positive change in the world.

Reflection

- Coming out of Ghost Mode – being more self-reflective, creating your Core Ideology, managing your ego, and learning to create connections – is like earning your black belt in Intentional Leadership. Then, the real work of mastery begins.
- Mastery of Intentional Leadership means doing three key things on an ongoing basis. I call these the Intentional Leadership Mastery Practices. They are:
  1. Ask for, receive, and integrate feedback.
  2. Consistently seek opportunities to improve.
  3. Become a teacher as well as a student.
- Too many people expect feedback to be perfectly worded, delivered at the right time, and contain instructions for how to become better. Most feedback is not gift-wrapped with an instruction manual. The person giving feedback is not responsible for teaching you how to integrate it.
- Intentional Leadership is not a theoretical practice; it's an experiential one. You can't just think about it. You must live it, embody it, and share it with others.

Unity of Thought and Action

Thought – focus on progress, not perfection

Congratulations on getting to this level in your leadership journey. If you have been incorporating the practices you've learned in this book, you have become skilled at being present, establishing trust, creating authenticity, and building unbreakable relationships.

Now, it's time to hone those skills by asking for feedback and then implementing changes to take your leadership to the next level.

Action – seek out feedback from others

Create a weekly practice to intentionally ask for feedback from someone in your network. When you have identified someone to ask, define what feedback you are looking to obtain. Send an advance copy of your questions and areas for feedback so the other person can prepare. Take time during the session to share how you are going to utilize the person's insights. (If the feedback is challenging, share the specific parts you are considering and commit to revisiting the conversation once you have an action plan.) It's recommended that you focus on one feedback session per week, for at least five consecutive weeks, to get the hang of this practice.

Here are some quick tips to get you started.

- **Make honesty easy.** Let the person providing feedback know that you appreciate honesty from them more than their attempts to protect your feelings.
- **Be prepared.** Before asking someone for feedback, plan and share questions with them so they can provide the greatest insight during your session.
- **Ask for clarity.** Not all feedback is easy to understand, so don't hesitate to ask them to clarify their point.
- **Avoid being hijacked.** The best way to kill any chance of regularly getting constructive feedback is to interrupt the person to defend yourself. If you're feeling hijacked, take deep breaths and keep listening.
- **Show appreciation.** Show that you appreciate the time you were given. Be thankful for feedback.

CHAPTER 9

A New World Vision for Leadership

'Great men are those who see that the spiritual is stronger than any material force – that thoughts rule the world.' – Emerson

While I was the CEO of Atrion, I had a senior leader who wanted to hire two additional staff because the workload had increased drastically with our company's growth over the previous 12 months. Unfortunately, because we were still navigating that expansion process, we weren't in a position to hire two additional overhead roles. So I challenged her to go back and rethink her position. What could she and her team do differently to get the job done without hiring additional people?

The truth was, I knew that her team wasn't working at capacity. They were punching the clock. They would come in at 8.00 a.m., then immediately start talking about their lunch breaks. They left precisely at 5.00p.m., regardless of whether they had completed the day's tasks. They weren't engaged. And since they were her direct reports, I encouraged her to find ways to engage them.

This manager and I got into a philosophical debate. She felt she was doing all she could to empower her team to be productive. I thought that we could energize this team to create more engagement, empowerment, and productivity. If done correctly, we might not have to increase our headcount by two staff members.

In the end, we decided to experiment. We would promote one of the individuals on the team to a team lead so she would have support in her efforts to engage her employees. I would guide this new leader in her new role and make myself accessible whenever she needed assistance.

The person we chose to promote was a woman named Grace. At first, she was reluctant to take on the role, but eventually she agreed. And within six months, she had created a whole new model of operations for this team.

As it turned out, there had been a lot of negativity happening in the department. I was aware of some of the issues, but the problem was more in-depth than I initially considered. The staff referred to themselves as 'The Mushrooms' – kept in the dark all day, unwanted and unimportant. Complaining was the standard mode of conversation. These employees felt isolated, underappreciated, and cut off from the rest of the company.

Those outside the department mirrored this attitude. When the sales team gave tours of our offices, they would often bypass the group, saying something to the effect of, 'Oh, that's just Fulfilment. Nothing to see there.'

It was true that Fulfilment wasn't a client-facing department. They were part of our Finance team, and their job was to initiate and manage the entire post-sales process. They handled purchasing, billing, scheduling, shipping, and myriad other 'back office' tasks. They were also responsible for cleaning up problems with clients in relation to contract and payment issues. In other words, they saw all the guts but none of the glory.

The senior leader who'd been urging me to hire more staff was doing her best, but she had limited time to spend with 'The Mushrooms' – and the time she did have was usually spent putting out fires and troubleshooting immediate issues.

Grace and I decided that, in order to turn the team around, she would need to shift the team's mindset. We had to find common ground in our shared values, purpose, and vision. To accomplish this goal, Grace scheduled a two-hour team meeting. Then, she created an exercise during which her team would identify everything they hated about their jobs. All the complaints would be written on a whiteboard. Only after everything was out in the open would she steer the discussion towards problem-solving.

For the first hour of the meeting, everyone got to vent. Lists were made of protocols and systems that were broken or outdated. Bottled-up resentment and frustrations were aired.

'I could tell everyone was feeling defeated,' Grace told me later. 'There was a *lot* of stuff on that whiteboard. It felt like everything was broken.'

But the second half of the meeting turned everything around. Grace asked the team to make a list of everything that they did daily: all the tasks they handled, all the systems they managed. All those 'boring' tasks such as invoicing, collections, purchasing, shipping and receiving, and other mundane duties went on to that whiteboard.

Then, she started asking, 'What happens if we don't do this correctly?' No one spoke.

'What if we don't invoice our clients?' she prompted.

'They don't pay their bills,' someone replied.

'And if they don't pay their bills?'

'We don't have cash coming in.'

'And if we don't have cash coming in?'

'We can't make payroll.' 'Exactly,' Grace nodded. 'And that affects every employee and their families. So … what about shipping? What happens if we don't take care of our tasks there?'

The team went on to make a list of all the ways in which their work made it possible for Atrion to exist. Grace stepped back and let them find all the places in which they had been making an impact without even realizing it.

Then, when the whiteboard was full and everyone was chattering excitedly, Grace retook the lead. 'So you see, our department is really at the centre of everything we do. If we don't function properly, neither does anyone else. We're like the heart in the human body. A body can live without a kidney or even a lung. But no one can live without a heart.'

From that day on, the Fulfilment department was no longer known as 'The Mushrooms'. Instead, they became 'The Heart of Atrion'.

The team dove into their work with a hugely renewed sense of purpose. Everything they did was for a greater good. They took the list of complaints from the first half of Grace's meeting and came up with simple solutions to resolve the issues. Complaining and negativity dropped to practically zero. Efficiency, output, and success rates skyrocketed. And although our company grew by 40 per cent that year, we didn't need to hire those two extra employees. The Heart of Atrion – now rebranded as the Logistics department – had become so effective that they kept up with everything and were asking for more.

In many organizations, our original situation would have been defined as a 'people problem' – meaning the team didn't have the right people to do the job. But what we really had – and what Grace's promotion and subsequent actions rectified – was a *leadership* problem. The original leader was stretched too thin, and couldn't be what the group needed in order to thrive.

What Grace did at that meeting is a perfect example of Intentional Leadership. Without changing a single thing about their jobs, she took her team from demoralized and resentful to engaged and purposeful. She empowered her department by giving them a voice and allowing them to exercise their judgement and creativity to create better solutions. Most of all, she showed her department that their work could be a source of pride, instead of merely a source of income.

It may seem like Grace did this effortlessly. But the truth is, that meeting was the result of many weeks of preparation, including her own self-awareness work. And when the moment came, she created a powerful shift because she approached the situation according to the Four Pillars of Intentional Leadership.

She was present for her team, and used that awareness to identify what was actually wrong (instead of merely what people were complaining about). She listened carefully, and acknowledged that their problems were real. Then, she took them through exercises that allowed them to become more self-aware and reflect on how they were engaging with the issues they'd identified. Instead of victims of circumstance, waiting for the proverbial knight in shining armour, they became motivated problem-solvers.

Next, she tapped into her inner authority and personal core values of connection and co-operation, and created a Core Ideology around what Fulfilment represented. Now, instead of sitting in the shadows, the team was able to see themselves as part of something greater. They took more responsibility, which strengthened their connection to the new Core Ideology.

Then, she empowered her team to make meaningful changes within their purview. She allowed them to solve the problems they'd been complaining about, along with the latitude to do so effectively.

Finally, Grace introduced a way for the team to become *connected* – to her, to each other, to their fellow Atrion employees and their families, and to a broader mission of service. They were no longer doing a 'back office' job. They were making sure that everyone at Atrion, their families, and the community continued to thrive.

Once the Four Pillars were in play, it was easy for The Heart of Atrion to set goals, create meaningful dialogue on a day-to-day basis, and come up with a system for feedback whereby everyone received the insights they needed to continually improve. The change became self-sustaining.

The most amazing part for me was that it all started with Grace's pure Unguarded Moment – the moment when she opened herself to the compelling vision of what her department was. When her team needed it most, she was able to let the perfect words flow in a state of real authenticity. That speech about Fulfilment being the heart of our company wasn't rehearsed. It wasn't premeditated. It came through her *at that moment* – and because we'd been working on the principles of Intentional Leadership (including creating stillness and Unguarded Moments) she was able to trust herself enough to let it flow. That five-minute speech changed the mindset of an entire department for many years to come.

My friend Orlando Bowen, keynote speaker and founder of One Voice, One Team says, 'We can't just raise the bar. We have to raise the floor.' Leaders stuck in Ghost Mode focus on raising the bar to improve performance. They establish new metrics and attempt to manage their team towards achievement. On the other hand, Intentional Leaders like Grace innovate ways to raise the floor – to make sure everyone rises together.

Everyone wants to belong to something. As the business landscape grows more competitive and our society grows more complex, this kind of connection will become even more vital to our success. The floor – the structure that bears the weight of the organization – can no longer look like the dingy, barely acceptable minimum. The top-down, hierarchical structure of the past no longer works.

We can do better. We *must* do better.

A group of people can do a job, or they can work for a purpose. They can be 'The Mushrooms' or they can be the beating heart of their organization. Intentional Leadership gives us the tools to create this kind of purposeful cohesion, engagement, and empowerment in our workplace through vision, values, and inspiration – and at the same time, generate record-breaking results.

As you've learned in this book, Intentional Leadership requires us to go above and beyond what is expected of us. It requires us to find and cultivate the leader within ourselves – to harness our unique strengths, overcome our reactivity, and become more each day than we were the day before.

The rise of the Intentional Leader

At the beginning of this book, we spoke about our current leadership crisis, and how too many people in power choose to sit back when they should stand up.

Ghost Mode is the reason why managers fail to lead, and leaders fail to compel. It's the reason why so many people in decision-making positions make the wrong calls, for the wrong reasons, and we all suffer the consequences. Poor leadership does more harm than good; just look at our global economic history over the last few decades! Banking crises, housing market crashes, corporate bailouts, insider trading, rampant discrimination, and sexual harassment … all of these events can be directly traced back to leadership mired in short-sighted greed, ego, and Ghost Mode. Because of the poor decisions of a relative few, hundreds of millions of lives were impacted negatively.

We can't go on like this.

The solution to our problems isn't to systemize decision-making (as many companies are trying to do). It's not more regulation, oversight, or layers of bureaucracy. It's to develop leaders who *know how to lead*. Leaders who have a clear vision and a deep connection to their inner authority. Leaders who will do the right thing without someone holding their feet to the fire. Leaders who will stand up to injustices, and refuse to engage in unethical and illegal behaviours. Leaders who are humble enough to admit their mistakes, and strive to do better next time. Leaders who are responsive instead of reactive. Leaders who lead by example, and create transformational relationships instead of transactional ones.

Most leadership models focus on skills and strategies; they're taught from the outside in. However, Intentional Leadership comes from the inside out; it's a reflection of what you have built inside yourself. As you've learned in this book, the only way to master this work is to practise it. It will get uncomfortable. It will be humbling. But if you are truly dedicated to leading the change in your company, your industry, or the world, it will all be worth it.

This book is your basic curriculum; your advanced studies are just beginning. The more you work with the Four Pillars, set goals for your Intentional Leadership, and cultivate opportunities for feedback, the more you will learn about yourself, your values, and your path as a leader. You will change, and keep changing. You will grow, and keep growing. And soon, you will find yourself rising into Defining and Decisive Moments in ways you never knew were possible.

Through this work, you will become more aware of who you are and what you stand for in the world. You will see your flaws more clearly, but judge them less. You will be accountable, and cease trying to justify your actions or play the victim when you've made a mistake. You will no longer think in polarities. You will become more than you were – and, in so doing, you will allow others to do the same.

As my friend Miguel says, 'We can *do* more because we *are* more. And if we can do more, we will eventually *have* more.'

You will make mistakes. Don't judge yourself too harshly. Intentional Leaders aren't perfect. They simply allow each error or imperfection to pull them closer to the ideal, rather than push them away from it.

The distance between who you are today and who you can become is called *virtue*. The more you narrow that gap, the more 'virtuous' you will become.

The waves will always be there. Sometimes, they will make it harder to see the horizon. Trust yourself to dive deep and find the currents instead. Be willing to see what others don't see, and go where others won't go. Cultivate your Unguarded Moments and be ready to let your greatness show itself. Stand up when you are needed, and lead from the front of the line.

I see a future where Intentional Leaders are transforming every industry – creating connection, empowerment, and growth on both micro and macro levels. A future where everyone is happy to do the job they've chosen. A future where people feel connected to their work, to one another, and to a greater good. A future where our health as a society is inextricably connected to our health in the workplace.

I see a future where we all rise together.

Will you join me?

Acknowledgements

It's been said that it takes a village to raise a child. It takes a city to write a book.

Our collective vision of the author as a solitary figure madly typing from some secluded location is the furthest thing from the truth. Don't get me wrong, there were moments of solitude and mad banging on my keyboard – but this process would not have been possible without the help of many hands.

First, I would like to recognize every single employee, client, and partner that graced our doors at Atrion. Our almost-30-year journey together created the crucible that melded my wild leadership ideals with their practical application. Thank you for your patience, understanding, belief, and (most importantly), your sometimes harsh but always loving criticism. A man could not have asked for better teachers, mentors, and friends. I love you.

I never really understood the work of an editor, and I cautiously selected Bryna Haynes. Bryna was a fierce collaborator. She helped shape the nature of the book, worked magic on the wording, and provided guidance and direction every step of the way. Not only that, she helped capture the voice and tone I was looking to create – no small task. *The Intentional Leader* wouldn't be a finished product without her.

Navigating the publishing world would have been impossible without Ken Lizotte and Elena Petricone at Emerson Consulting. For over 10 years, Ken has been encouraging me to write this book. He believed in my vision of leadership and the message I had to share. It wasn't a straight-line journey, but Ken secured a publishing deal with Bloomsbury Publishing Plc. What an incredibly supportive team! Thanks to Matt, Allie, and all of the editors and designers who helped bring this book to life.

Thanks to my team of beta readers and proofreaders who helped get this book across the finish line! Kim Hebert, Erica Davies, David Roache, Miguel Rey, Carole Ann Penny, David Braid, and JoAnn Johnson, your diligence allowed me to hit every deadline without looking like a fool.

Finally, I am deeply grateful for the love and support of my wife Kim for the last 33 years. In 2021 Kim lost a short but hard-fought battle with pancreatic cancer. She always inspired me to be a better man, husband, father, leader, and human. Throughout our marriage, we learned the value of living in and for the moment. It was through these pure Unguarded Moments that the seeds of *The Intentional Leader* took hold. Kim, thank you for listening to me drone on about leadership, intentionality, and the unguarded moment. Your patience and grace knew no bounds as you listened to one story after another, helped to facilitate yet another leadership program, and read page after page of this manuscript. To infinity and beyond, plus one.

About the Author

Tim O. Hebert

At age three, Tim had all the characteristics needed to become a successful superhero: high energy, a strong moral compass, a burning desire to have an impact on the world, and a devout admiration for the greatest superhero of all time, Wolverine.

Somewhere along the way – and after many failed attempts to fly – Tim learned that his superpower wasn't beating up villains. It was empowering the 'good guys' by igniting the leadership spark in those around him.

As a business owner, national speaker, workshop facilitator, and published author, Tim has explored and defined the principles surrounding Intentional Leadership over the past three decades. As CEO and President of Atrion, a leading IT services firm, he grew this company to $168 million with more than 260 employees. His organization was centred on strong, vibrant culture, empowered employees, and fanatical passion for excellence.

Under Tim's tenure, Atrion became an employer of choice, named one of Rhode Island's 'Best Places to Work' companies for seven straight years. Atrion was recognized on the Inc. 5000 List of fastest-growing private companies for eight years in a row and was a perennial on CRN's Fastest Growing Companies and Top Managed Service Providers (MSP) List.

Currently, Tim serves as CEO and Founder of Trilix, a cutting-edge business and technology consulting firm. He uses his superpowers to activate new beliefs about leadership in audiences around the US. In short, Tim helps his audiences develop into Intentional Leaders.

Tim has facilitated workshops at major companies including Cisco, USRobotics, Assumption College, Rhode Island Quality Institute, National Marker Corporation, Town Dock, Packeteer, Panduit, and Banco de Brazil, among others. He has also spoken on the topics of Intentional Leadership, culture, and change at dozens of symposiums and conferences, including NERCOMP's annual conference, SUNY, Tech Collective, InService, NEAP, SHRM, and SIM meet-ups. He has also created many successful events, including his annual ON Leadership Symposium and the Always ON Symposium. His published works have appeared on IDG Contributor Network, BTOES Insights, Channel Reseller, and CRN, among others.

He has also taken significant leadership roles as a mentor through The Academy of Career Exploration, a Trustee for the Rhode Island Public Expenditure Council, a Director of the Rhode Island Commerce Corporation, and a board member for several non-profits, including Boy Scouts of America-Narragansett Council, Tech Collective, and Rhode Island Museum of Science and Art (RIMOSA). Tim has also served his country as a member of the United States Air Force.

When he isn't busy speaking, writing, and running several companies, you'll find Tim seeking out his next big climb (South America is next), hopping on a plane to explore someplace new and making sure his office mini-fridge of Diet Coke is always stocked.

Recommended Reading

The 4 Disciplines of Execution: Achieving Your Wildly Important Goals by Chris McChesney, Sean Covey, and Jim Huling

The Advantage: Why Organizational Health Trumps Everything Else In Business by Patrick M. Lencioni

Good to Great: Why Some Companies Make the Leap and Others Don't by Jim Collins

Great by Choice: Uncertainty, Chaos, and Luck–Why Some Thrive Despite Them All by Jim Collins and Morten T. Hansen

A More Beautiful Question: The Power of Inquiry to Spark Breakthrough Ideas by Warren Berger

Start with Why: How Great Leaders Inspire Everyone to Take Action by Simon Sinek

Emotional Intelligence: Why It Can Matter More Than IQ by Daniel Goleman

The Oz Principle: Getting Results Through Individual and Organizational Accountability by Roger Connors, Tom Smith, Craig Hickman

Delivering Happiness: A Path to Profit, Passion, and Purpose by Tony Hsieh

PEAK: How Great Companies Get Their Mojo from Maslow Revised and Updated by Chip Conley and Tony Hsieh

Mindset: The New Psychology of Success by Carol S. Dweck

Daring Greatly: How the Courage to Be Vulnerable Transforms the Way We Live, Love, Parent, and Lead by Brené Brown

Speed of Trust: The One Thing That Changes Everything by Stephen M. R. Covey

Index